BRAND-AS-A-PLATFORM

REVENUE SUBSCRIBED

ALGORITHMIC FIRST

NARRATIVES

DESIGNING CUSTOMERS, NOT PRODUCTS

B.R.A.N.D

FUTURE PROOFING FOR THE ALGORITHMIC ERA

RANGHAN VENKATRAMAN

notionpress.com

INDIA • SINGAPORE • MALAYSIA

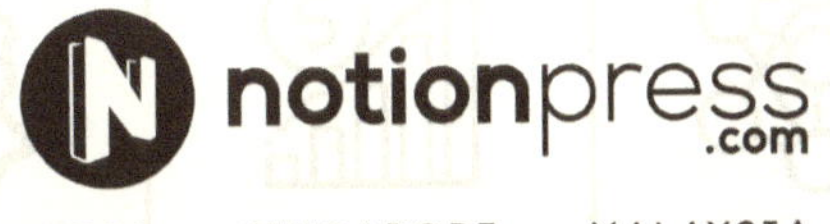

ISBN 979-8-89186-341-5

Literary Light: Illuminating Paths for Autism and Underprivileged Kids

With your purchase of this book, you're not just gaining a treasure of knowledge but also contributing to a noble cause. The proceeds are allocated to Spectrum Spotlight, a non-profit organization focused on autism, and towards supporting underprivileged children with special needs. This gesture of yours extends beyond reading, directly impacting lives and fostering positive change in our community.

Contents

Foreword

In 'B.R.A.N.D. Unleashed,' the author Ranghan presents more than just a book; it's a dynamic exploration into the heart of enterprise creation in the AI era. This work goes beyond traditional texts, delving deep into the intricacies of modern business strategy with an expert touch. Each page is alive with innovative ideas and memorable insights, such as 'Brands are defined not just by products, but by the stories that resonate with consumers.' Ranghan skillfully unfolds these narratives, offering profound knowledge and a compelling invitation to reshape the future of branding.

Imagine yourself as a business leader, steering through the changing market currents with the B.R.A.N.D. framework as your guide, and consider the vast potential for growth and innovation that lies ahead. The book's strength is its holistic, interdisciplinary approach, blending digital and data-centric thinking with intricate financial models like subscription revenue and cost analysis. This blend extends beyond theory, offering practical, real-world guidance for leaders across various industries.

In summary, this book is an invitation to not only gain knowledge but to experience an AI era transformative journey.

Madhu Ranganathan

CFO, OpenText | Board Member, Akamai

Preface: Crafting a Symphony of Differentiation

Central Idea: Orchestrating Brand Differentiation

At the heart of "B.R.A.N.D." is a revelation: winning in today's market is akin to conducting a symphony where every business element, from the subtlest brand nuance to the boldest customer engagement strategy, plays its part in a larger, more intricate composition. This book is a tribute to the art of differentiation, teaching you to weave these diverse elements into a distinctive and harmonious brand presence that captures and holds the market's attention. Here, in "B.R.A.N.D.," we dare to challenge the status quo, inviting entrepreneurs who seek not just to play in the market, but to conduct a masterpiece of success.

Why Immerse Yourself in B.R.A.N.D.?

1. **Understanding the New Business Dynamics:** In a world where change is the only constant, this book serves as your compass, helping you navigate the ever-evolving business landscape with agility and foresight.

2. **Mastering Brand Differentiation:** Learn the delicate art of setting your brand apart in a world teeming with noise. It's about striking the right chord with your audience, creating a unique brand symphony that resonates with depth and authenticity.

3. **Purposeful Innovation:** Here, innovation isn't a buzzword; it's a heartfelt melody. You'll discover how to innovate with intention, creating products and services that forge meaningful and lasting connections with your audience.

4. **The Magic of Storytelling:** Uncover the power of narrative in branding. Learn how to craft compelling brand stories that engage, inspire, and create an emotional resonance with your audience.

5. **Data-Driven Decisions with Soul:** Data isn›t just a tool; it›s the rhythm of your brand›s heartbeat. Embrace data-driven strategies that personalize and elevate customer experiences while retaining a human touch.

6. **Crafting Experiences, Not Just Products:** Shift your focus from mere products to creating immersive experiences. Like a skilled composer, design every customer interaction to leave a lasting, harmonious impression.

The Movements of B.R.A.N.D.: A Guide to Masterful Brand Conducting

1. **Brand-as-a-Platform:** Step into a world where brands are living, breathing platforms of engagement. This part guides you in creating authentic connections, adapting dynamically to audience feedback, and conducting a brand narrative that resonates across various channels.

2. **Revenue: A Sonata of Subscription Harmony:** Dive into the rhythm of sustainable revenue models. Explore the nuances of subscription-based models and learn how to create a seamless blend of recurring revenue streams that harmonize with customer needs and expectations.

3. **Algorithmic First: The Data-Concerto:** In this data-driven age, algorithms are your maestro›s wand, guiding you to tailor customer experiences with precision. Discover how to use data to anticipate needs, personalize interactions, and orchestrate a customer journey that is as fluid as it is captivating.

4. **Narrative Brands: Emotional Melodies in Branding:** Here, you›ll delve into the art of storytelling, where brands

transcend the transactional to touch the heart. Learn to weave stories that not only narrate your brand›s journey but also resonate with the emotional chords of your audience.

5. **Designing for Customers: A Crescendo of Experiences:** Conclude your journey by learning how to design not just products but memorable customer experiences. This section teaches you to think like a composer, envisioning and crafting each interaction to leave an indelible mark on your audience›s hearts and minds.

Embarking on Your Symphony of Success

As you turn the pages of "B.R.A.N.D.," consider yourself at the podium of your business, baton in hand, ready to conduct a symphony of brand differentiation. Each part, each insight, is a step toward mastering the nuanced art of standing out in business. Your entrepreneurial journey is a canvas awaiting your masterpiece - a blend of innovation, strategy, and emotional resonance.

Welcome to the world of "B.R.A.N.D.," where the art of business is not just about playing the game but about creating a symphony that echoes in the halls of market success. Here, you're not just an entrepreneur; you're a maestro of your unique brand symphony, playing to win in the grand concerto of entrepreneurship.

Preview: A Symphony of Differentiation

In the ever-evolving theater of business, where yesterday's strategies fade into the backdrop of history, the art of entrepreneurship has transformed into an intricate symphony of adaptation and innovation. Entrepreneurs and even large enterprises today find themselves center stage, under the spotlight of consumer scrutiny, where every note they play must resonate harmoniously with the ever-changing desires of a dynamic audience.

Entrepreneurs and even large enterprises today find themselves center stage, under the spotlight of consumer scrutiny, where every note they play must resonate stage. The notes before you are not static; they're the potential to craft a symphony of experiences that extend far beyond the point of purchase. Each decision you make, each strategy you implement, contributes to the symphony you're composing – one that will resonate not only in the present but also in the echoes of the future.

Just as the composition of a symphony requires an intricate understanding of the interplay between individual notes and the overall harmony, building brands that stand out in a crowded marketplace demands a masterful touch. In this age of rapid change, creating brands that capture the current zeitgeist while remaining immune to the dissonance of shifting trends necessitates an approach that goes beyond the conventional.

Welcome to an orchestration of brands that dares to be different. This is an invitation to join the ranks of visionary conductors of our time, individuals who navigate the complexities of business with the creative finesse of a symphony composer. Each section of this symphony represents a movement, a harmonious blend of insights, lessons, anecdotes, and counterintuitive analyses – much like the cadence of notes in a symphony.

Crafting a Symphony of Differentiation

As you embark on this symphonic journey, envision yourself as the conductor guiding the orchestra. Each part, like a movement, contributes to the composition of your brand's future. The insights, lessons from triumphant symphonies and poignant ones, all contribute to your role as the conductor of a next-generation brand. Let the resonance of your brand symphony echo not only in the notes of today but throughout the harmonious melodies of generations yet to come.

Part 1: Brand-as-a-Platform - An Overture of Evolution

As you raise the baton, anticipate the grandeur of our opening movement, an overture that will set the tone for the symphony ahead. Our journey commences with the contemplation of brands in the modern era – dynamic entities that have transcended the confines of mere labels. They've evolved into vibrant platforms that stretch their reach to form communities of enthusiasts, orchestrating an intricate dance of engagement, connection, and evolution.

In this movement, envision yourself as a conductor who interacts with the audience, senses their reactions, and adapts the tempo accordingly. Similarly, modern brands must engage in a dialogue with their audience, responding to their cues and adapting strategies based on real-time feedback. This interaction transforms brands from monologues to dynamic conversations, echoing the transformation of brands from static labels to living platforms.

Authenticity becomes your conductor's baton, guiding the interactions, collaborations, and engagements that take place on the brand's stage. Like a symphony conductor's gestures inspiring musicians to blend their unique tones into a harmonious whole, your brand's authenticity inspires customers, collaborators, and enthusiasts to align their values, creating a symphony of resonance that reverberates far and wide.

Part 2: Revenue - A Sonata of Subscription Harmony

As the second movement begins, imagine a sonata building in intensity. In this movement, we venture into the realm of revenue, where the conventional rhythm of transactions is replaced by the captivating cadences of subscriptions. Subscriptions, much like recurring motifs in a symphony, create an ongoing engagement that harmonizes business and customer.

Just as a sonata weaves intricate melodies, your exploration of revenue will harmonize the dance between businesses and customers through the captivating rhythm of subscription models. Case studies will be the melodies of lessons, highlighting both triumphs and pitfalls. Just as a sonata showcases different themes and motifs, these case studies will present diverse perspectives, contributing to the symphony of lessons that shape the rhythm of sustainable revenue generation.

Part 3: Algorithmic First - A Concerto of Data-Driven Harmony

As we progress to the third movement, envision a concerto where data and insights orchestrate the symphony. Algorithms, much like a conductor's cues, anticipate customer preferences and curate personalized narratives. The movement delves into algorithmic innovation, where data guides the creation of tailored experiences that captivate individuals yet resonate universally.

Imagine each algorithmic cue as a note in a concerto, creating a fluid and dynamic choreography. Algorithmic-first thinking becomes a counterintuitive approach, where data guides the creation of symphonies of tailored experiences. Algorithms predict desires, analyze trends, and craft personalized stories that resonate universally, similar to the motifs that recur throughout a concerto.

Part 4: Narrative Brands - Crafting Melodies of Emotional Connection

In the fourth movement, imagine a chamber orchestra weaving a tapestry of emotions through melodies. This movement reveals the power of storytelling to create connections that echo long after the final note fades. Narrative brands use the art of storytelling to weave intricate threads of emotions, experiences, and values. These narratives tap into emotional chords, resonating far beyond the transactional.

Just as a conductor conveys emotions through the sincerity of performance, narrative brands captivate through authenticity. Authentic narratives forge a genuine bond between brands and customers, much like a chamber orchestra creates emotional resonance through its melodies.

Part 5: Design Customers, not Products - Orchestrating Harmonious Experiences

In the final movement, your journey culminates in designing harmonious experiences. This movement focuses on customer-centric design, where interactions anticipate needs and create lasting impressions. Designing customer-centric experiences is akin to shaping melodies that resonate deeply. Just as a composer envisions the lasting impact of a symphony, you'll envision the longevity of your design choices.

This symphony of differentiation is your opportunity to conduct a brand that stands apart, a brand that resonates with authenticity, innovation, and emotional connection. Each section of this symphony is a movement in the composition of your brand's legacy, a legacy that will resound through time. As you embrace the wisdom and shape your symphony, remember that you are not merely an entrepreneur; you are a conductor of a brand that dares to be different, a brand that orchestrates a symphony of success in a world of constant change.

Embark on Your Symphony of Success

The stage is set, a grand theater of possibilities awaits, and you stand at its center, ready to embark on a symphonic journey of entrepreneurship like no other. Just as a maestro takes the podium before an eager orchestra, you step into the spotlight as the conductor of your brand's destiny. With every page turned and every concept embraced, you're poised to create a masterpiece that will resonate through time.

As you raise your baton, envision the rhythm of innovation and adaptation as the foundation of your symphony. The tempo is not fixed; it adapts, accelerates, and evolves in harmony with the ever-changing landscapes of business and consumer desires. Your role as a conductor transcends transactional pursuits; you're here to compose experiences, to craft a narrative that extends beyond individual notes, and to create resonance that echoes through generations.

Harmonizing Innovation: Crafting Your Entrepreneurial Overture

In the realm of entrepreneurship, just as a composer molds melodies to build an overture, you will craft your entrepreneurial overture. The keys before you are not static; they are dynamic, representing the products and services that you orchestrate into a harmonious composition. As you press each key, you're not just creating for the moment but for a symphony that will enthrall the audience of the future.

Much like the interplay of notes in an overture, your journey is one of finding the perfect balance between individual elements and the complete melody. As the maestro of your entrepreneurial endeavor, you'll blend innovation, adaptation, and foresight to compose a symphony that resounds with the needs and aspirations of your audience.

The Crescendo of Brand Evolution: Crafting a Harmonious Movement

In the first movement, the concept of brand-as-a-platform takes center stage. Imagine stepping into the shoes of a conductor who engages with the audience, senses their reactions, and adjusts the tempo accordingly. Likewise, modern brands engage with their audience through dialogue, adapting their strategies based on real-time feedback. This movement isn't just about labels; it's about creating a living, breathing platform that nurtures connections, orchestrates experiences, and evolves with authenticity.

Authenticity, the conductor's baton, guides your interactions, just as it guides a symphony. Your brand-as-a-platform resonates through the authenticity it nurtures within its community. Like the harmony of a symphony, this authenticity inspires alignment and connection, creating a symphony of resonance that reverberates far and wide.

Crafting the Sonata of Revenue Generation: Building a Harmonious Bridge

In the second movement, the melody of revenue generation takes center stage. Picture this movement as a sonata, gradually building in intensity. Just as a sonata weaves intricate melodies, your exploration of revenue harmonizes the dance between businesses and customers through the captivating rhythm of subscription models. Subscriptions become recurring motifs that thread through your revenue strategy, creating an ongoing engagement that harmonizes business and customer.

Real business examples become the melodies of lessons, offering insights from both triumphs and pitfalls. Much like a sonata showcases different themes and motifs, these case studies present diverse perspectives, contributing to the symphony of lessons that shape the rhythm of sustainable revenue generation. As you delve into these lessons, you learn to strike the balance between value and loyalty, just as a conductor balances instruments to create a resonant symphony.

The Concerto of Algorithmic Innovation: Crafting Data-Driven Harmonies

As we move to the third movement, envision a concerto where algorithms take the place of the conductor. Data and insights orchestrate this concerto, guiding customer experiences much like a conductor guides an orchestra. This movement explores algorithmic innovation, where data-driven insights anticipate preferences and curate personalized narratives.

Imagine each algorithmic cue as a note in a concerto, creating a fluid and dynamic choreography. Algorithmic-first thinking becomes a counterintuitive approach, where data guides the creation of symphonies of tailored experiences. Algorithms predict desires, analyze trends, and craft personalized stories that resonate universally, like the motifs that recur throughout a concerto.

Crafting the Emotional Symphony of Narrative Brands: Weaving Stories of Connection

In the fourth movement, the spotlight shifts to narrative brands, akin to a chamber orchestra weaving a tapestry of emotions through melodies. Stories transcend words and evolve into emotional symphonies that linger in the hearts of customers. This movement reveals the power of storytelling to create connections that echo long after the final note fades.

Narrative brands use the art of storytelling to weave intricate threads of emotions, experiences, and values. These narratives tap into emotional chords, resonating far beyond the transactional. As you immerse yourself in this movement, you'll uncover how authentic narratives forge a genuine bond between brands and customers. Like a conductor conveying emotions through the sincerity of performance, narrative brands captivate through authenticity.

Designing Harmonious Experiences: Creating Your Final Crescendo

In the final movement, your journey culminates in designing harmonious experiences. Imagine the entire orchestra uniting in a powerful chorus, much like your brand's interactions harmonizing into memorable experiences. This movement focuses on customer-centric design, where interactions anticipate needs and create lasting impressions.

Designing customer-centric experiences is akin to shaping melodies that resonate deeply. Just as a composer envisions the lasting impact of a symphony, you'll envision the longevity of your design choices. These experiences become your final crescendo, ensuring resonance not only with present but also future generations of customers.

Compose Your Masterpiece: Embrace the Wisdom and Shape Your Legacy

As the symphony draws to a close, remember that you are the conductor of your entrepreneurial journey. Each part, each movement, contributes to the composition of your brand's symphony. The insights gained, the lessons learned, and the melodies of triumph and failure all contribute to your role as the conductor of a next-generation brand.

You stand on the cusp of greatness, poised to compose a brand symphony that resonates through the ages. The symphony of your brand will echo not only in the notes of today but throughout the harmonious melodies of generations yet to come. Embrace the wisdom, shape your legacy, and lead your brand to a resounding crescendo of success. Your symphony awaits – let the music begin.

A Tribute to 'Different' by Youngme Moon: The Muse Behind 'B.R.A.N.D.'

Discovering 'Different':

My journey to writing "B.R.A.N.D." began in the vibrant pages of Youngme Moon's book "Different." Moon's insightful exploration of the unconventional and the celebration of divergence from the norm struck a profound chord with me. Her ability to delve deep into the heart of what makes a brand stand out in a sea of sameness illuminated my path. It was in her thought-provoking analysis and her challenge to the status quo that the seeds for "B.R.A.N.D." were sown.

First Movement: Embracing Uniqueness

"Different" taught me the power of uniqueness in a world often clouded by conformity. This principle became the foundation of "B.R.A.N.D.," where I explore the notion of brand-as-a-platform. Like Moon's encouragement to step away from competitive herd behavior, I advocate for a dialogue-based approach where brands and consumers co-create value. Moon's perspective on differentiation not just as a strategy but as an ethos, resonates through every part of my book.

Second Movement: The Symphony of Disruption

Youngme Moon's portrayal of 'idea brands' as disruptors reshaped my understanding of market dynamics. This inspired the 'Sonata of Revenue Generation' in "B.R.A.N.D.," where I correlate revenue strategies with the disruptive power of innovation. Just as Moon celebrates the brands that rewrite rules, I emphasize how innovative revenue models can redefine customer relationships and market engagement.

Third Movement: Data as a Differentiator

The influence of "Different" is particularly evident in the 'Concerto of Algorithmic Innovation' in my book. Moon's insights into how brands can break away from traditional molds inspired my exploration of algorithmic innovation as a means of crafting personalized customer experiences. Her emphasis on the unique over the uniform guides my discussion on using data not just for optimization, but for creating distinct and memorable brand stories.

Fourth Movement: Storytelling and Emotional Connect

Moon's emphasis on the emotional connection that differentiates successful brands directly inspired the 'Emotional Symphony of Narrative Brands' in "B.R.A.N.D." Her perspective on the power of storytelling and creating a bond beyond the product ignited my exploration into how narrative brands can weave stories that resonate deeply with their audience, creating lasting emotional symphonies.

Fifth Movement: Crafting Lasting Impressions

"Different" concludes with an emphasis on lasting impact, a theme I echo in the 'Crescendo of Experience Design' in my work. Moon's advocacy for brands that leave a lasting impression inspired me to emphasize the importance of designing customer experiences that not only resonate today but also echo into the future, much like the enduring impact of a well-composed symphony.

Epilogue: A Harmonious Legacy

In "Different," Youngme Moon provided a lens through which I could view the world of branding in a new light. This book has been more than just an inspiration; it has been a guide and a muse. In "B.R.A.N.D.," I strive to build on Moon's revolutionary ideas, offering my own interpretation and extension of her groundbreaking concepts. As Moon has illuminated the path to differentiation, I aim to illuminate the path to building a brand that not only stands out but sings out, in a symphony of innovation and authenticity.

PART-1

BRAND-AS-A-PLATFORM

THE FOUNDATION OF IDENTITY

The Foundation of Identity

In the bustling heart of the city, amidst the towering skyscrapers and neon lights, a transformation is underway—one that transcends the traditional boundaries of business and branding. Imagine walking through these streets, where every storefront, every advertisement, and every interaction feels different, almost surreal.

Welcome to a world where brands are no longer content to merely exist; they aspire to become something more—a platform for stories, experiences, and connections.

Step into the shoes of Alex, a young professional navigating this evolving landscape. One day, Alex finds herself drawn to an enigmatic door, standing out against the backdrop of ordinary storefronts. Emboldened by curiosity, she pushes it open, and what she discovers within defies everything she thought she knew about brands.

This isn't just a store; it's a universe. The walls are adorned with vivid murals that seem to come alive, telling tales of adventure, community, and purpose. The air is electric with the hum of conversation as people gather, not just to buy products, but to immerse themselves in something more profound—an experience that resonates with their aspirations.

As Alex explores further, she encounters stations where customers engage with interactive displays, sharing their own stories, visions, and creativity. This isn't a mere exchange of goods; it's a dialogue, a dynamic exchange where the brand listens as much as it speaks. The brand isn't just selling products; it's building connections, one interaction at a time.

In a corner of the space, Alex stumbles upon a screen displaying a montage of moments—ordinary people's lives intersecting with the brand's journey. Each story represents a partnership, a shared narrative, and an invitation to be part of something bigger than oneself. As the stories unfold, Alex realizes that these aren't just customers; they're collaborators, shaping the brand's identity as much as it shapes theirs.

Exiting the space, Alex isn't just leaving a store; she's stepping out of the ordinary into a realm of possibilities. The brand has transformed from a static entity into a vibrant platform—a platform that invites participation, co-creation, and belonging. It's a world where commerce merges with community, and where the boundaries between brand and consumer blur.

As we embark on this journey through the parts ahead, we invite you to explore the intricacies, innovations, and inspirations that define this new era of branding. Just as Alex's experience illustrates, the transformation from Brand-as-a-Product to Brand-as-a-Platform is a shift that promises not just a change in strategy, but a change in perspective—a reimagining of what brands can be and the connections they can forge.

Welcome to the world of Brand-as-a-Platform—a realm where brands transcend traditional boundaries and become catalysts for connection, empowerment, and transformation. Just as Alex's experience demonstrates, this isn't about products; it's about possibilities. As we delve into the parts ahead, we'll explore the intricacies, inspirations, and insights that define this new era of branding.

This isn't merely a segment of this book; it's a gateway to a realm where brands transcend mere symbols and merchandise. Prepare yourself as we journey through the intricacies of the Brand Platform Blueprint, a guide that aims to transform your perception of branding and welcomes you to be part of a movement that focuses equally on individuals and products.

An Extraordinary Evolution

In a world where brands are more than logos and products, they've transformed into something extraordinary—a platform. This platform is deeper than appearances, inviting us to explore, join, and co-create. Envision a stage where the audience isn't mere spectators; they're active participants, influencers, and even scriptwriters. Welcome to the era of Brand-as-a-Platform, where engagement rules are rewritten, and the concept of being a brand takes on a new meaning.

A Gateway Beyond Ordinary

Imagine closing your eyes and stepping onto a platform that defies the ordinary. The ground beneath you pulses with life, responding to your presence. Each step is accompanied by a subtle warmth, and the air thrums with anticipation. You're no longer an observer; you're an active participant, co-creating an unfolding narrative. This isn't just a stage; it's an entrance to a realm where brands shed their static forms to become dynamic platforms.

A Journey, Not Just a Transaction

Picture this: You're not merely purchasing a product or service; you're stepping onto a platform that calls you to join a journey. This isn't a cold, faceless entity; it's a dynamic stage where connections are forged, stories are woven, and experiences are curated. Visualize brands as directors of their narratives, inviting you, the audience, to do more than watch—to become engaged participants. Welcome to Brand-as-a-Platform, the threshold to a new dimension of branding.

Breaking Free from the Past

This transformation mirrors the dawn of a new era, where brands break free from traditional marketing constraints. It's akin to a caterpillar weaving a cocoon, only to emerge as a vibrant butterfly.

Brand-as-a-Platform redefines engagement, urging consumers to transcend mere purchases and embrace belonging, interaction, and active participation in shaping the narrative.

Vibrant Interactions in a Marketplace

Imagine your online experience not as a scroll, but as a bustling marketplace where every click resonates with purpose. As you navigate, voices from all directions echo—the collective wisdom of users sharing experiences, forming connections. This isn't a monologue; it's a dialogue, a symphony of interactions composing a grand opus.

Empowerment Through User-Generated Content

Consider a cosmetics brand's platform—it's not solely about product advertisements. It's a space where users share makeup tutorials, reviews, and their own beauty transformations. The brand's evolution surpasses selling makeup; it's a platform empowering customer to showcase creativity and skills, fostering a vibrant community of beauty enthusiasts.

Journey Beyond Accommodations

Airbnb's platform isn't just about booking lodgings; it's about immersing yourself in a new way of life. Hosts sharing stories about their homes, neighborhoods, and local experiences weave a tapestry of connections beyond transactions. Airbnb transcends being a lodging service; it's a platform fostering cultural exchange, transforming travelers into temporary locals. Welcome to the realm of Brand-as-a-Platform.

Brand as Masterful Directors

Envision brands as masterful directors, not merely presenting a story, but inviting you to assume a leading role. This isn't passive; it's a symphony of interactions where your actions shape the narrative. The spotlight isn't on the brand alone; it's shared with you, the participant, at the intersection of experience and engagement. The excitement is tangible, akin to the energy before a curtain rises—your pivotal role in the evolving tale of Brand-as-a-Platform.

Engaging in a Living Narrative

Imagine the hush as the first notes of a symphony fill a concert hall. Similarly, the air buzzes with anticipation as you step onto this metaphorical stage. The world around you shimmers with potential, every interaction a note in the symphony of your brand journey. Your footsteps resonate on the digital landscape, harmonizing with fellow participants in this grand spectacle.

The Evolution of Branding: From Products to Platforms

The Brand Odyssey: From Product Monologues to Platform Dialogues

Embark on a journey through the annals of branding, a voyage back to a time tinted in sepia tones. Here, in the storied corridors of traditional brand strategy, brands stood as soloists, their voices echoing in a chorus of product praises. This was an era illuminated by logos, catchy jingles, and the allure of a better life through consumption. The narrative was simple, almost charming in its straightforwardness: "Here's our product, here's what it does, and here's why it belongs with you." This part of our odyssey waltzes through these nostalgic days, dusting off the age-old playbooks, shining a light on the direct, product-focused branding that once dominated the market.

Fast-forward to the present and witness a dramatic metamorphosis in the world of branding. In this contemporary epoch, brands have evolved from solitary performers to orchestrators of grand, experiential symphonies. This is the dawning of platform-based branding, a dazzling spectrum where brands transcend their physical offerings to forge realms of engagement, emotion, and profound connection.

In this vibrant new landscape, brands engage in a dialogue, not a monologue. They're not merely selling; they're enchanting, weaving narratives that captivate and resonate. This dance between brands and consumers is powered by digital innovation, fostering deeper, more meaningful connections. We delve into the heart of this transformation, exploring how brands have metamorphosed from mere product providers to architects of ecosystems pulsating with interaction, personalization, and co-creation.

We'll navigate the fusion of data and narrative, the crafting of communities, and the creation of experiences that linger in memory, eclipsing the mere features of products. This is a tale of evolution, of branding shedding its old skin to reveal a form that's more responsive, agile, and empathetic. A form that speaks with the consumer in a language rich in possibilities and promise.

Join us as we trace not just the evolution of branding but a revolution in how brands connect, communicate, and create value. Welcome to the era of platform-based branding, a realm that's as much about crafting dreams and forging relationships as it is about products and profits.

In the grand gallery of modern commerce, brands stand as chameleons, ever transforming from their cocoons of simplicity into vibrant butterflies of complexity. This metamorphosis mirrors the rhythmic changes of our society, transcending the ordinary transaction. It's a shift from the monochromatic "buy this product" to a kaleidoscope of "join our story." Observe Patagonia, not just an outdoor apparel brand, but a clarion call to environmental activism, intertwining the threads of their garments with narratives of ecological stewardship.

Brands have transcended mere monologues; they've become symphonies, rich with emotion, rhythm, and harmony. In this orchestra, each brand, like Disney, emerges as a maestro, orchestrating experiences that transcend the bounds of time and space, inviting audiences to not just hear a story but to live it. This is branding in stereo, a dimensional leap from the flatlands of features and benefits to the rich tapestry of immersive experiences.

In this dance of dialogue, consumers, and brands step onto the floor as partners. Lego, for example, transforms its enthusiasts into architects, empowering them to shape the very products they cherish. This is no longer a simple exchange of demand and supply; it's a tango of co-creation, a dynamic interplay of ideas and inspirations.

Brands now curate not just tangible products: they are custodians of intangible realms. Starbucks, more than a mere coffee shop, is a sanctuary, a 'third place' imbued with aromas and ambiance, where each sip brews a narrative, and every corner cradles a conversation. This illustrates how brands can become integral threads in the social fabric, seamlessly weaving themselves into our daily lives.

And in this evolving narrative, technology acts as the loom. Brands like Nike are interlacing digital threads – AR, VR, AI – into their tapestry, transforming traditional transactions into immersive journeys of discovery. This isn't mere personalization; it's the opening of gateways to new worlds, where every interaction paints a stroke on the canvas of customer experience.

The branding of today is a rich mosaic, a multidimensional space where products, stories, and experiences intertwine. It's no longer just a billboard but a landscape, no longer a slogan but a living story, and no longer a transaction but a journey. In this world, brands are not just observed; they are experienced, lived, and co-authored. This is the new art of branding – a canvas where each color, line, and texture contribute to a larger, more vibrant picture.

In this new art of branding, the story has evolved from a monochromatic narrative of product features to a rich tapestry of experiences, emotions, and engagements. Brands are no longer mere entities; they are universes to be explored, stories to be lived, and odysseys to be co-authored. It's a canvas where every hue, line, and texture converge to create a vibrant masterpiece, as alive and dynamic as the audience it captivates. This is not just branding; it's a creation of worlds, an art form where the brand and consumer together paint the future in vivid, resonant colors.

Building a Brand Ecosystem

A Multidimensional Mansion

Orchestrating Harmony: The Pillars of a Brand Ecosystem

Embark on an odyssey into the world of brand ecosystems, akin to an artist weaving a masterpiece on a vast canvas. This narrative explores the intricate balance between the tangible aspects of products and services and the intangible elements of brand ethos, values, and culture. It's a journey through the alchemy of fusing innovative design, exceptional service, and compelling content with cutting-edge technology to cultivate a dynamic brand ecosystem.

Envision this ecosystem as a living entity, where every component – from customer engagement strategies to community building – interplays harmoniously. Each aspect is a color on the artist's palette, blending to create an image that captivates and resonates. Here, brands breathe life into their ecosystems, transforming every interaction into a meaningful encounter, painting a picture that extends far beyond the conventional boundaries of business.

Weaving the Fabric of Experiences

Step into the realm of integrated brand storytelling, where the lines between products, services, and experiences blur into a seamless and enchanting narrative. In this world, a brand's offerings transcend mere functionality; they become chapters in an ongoing story, with customers as the protagonists.

Picture a brand ecosystem as an orchestral symphony, where each element – from product innovation to customer service –

harmonizes to produce a melody that echoes in the hearts of the audience. This section celebrates the conductors of the brand world, those who masterfully orchestrate these elements, creating ecosystems that are symphonies of engagement and connection.

Here, we confront the complexities of integrating these diverse elements, ensuring they sing in unison. It's about more than alignment; it's about creating a narrative where each business unit, each product, each service, contributes to a cohesive and immersive brand experience. This journey is about brands evolving into entities that are greater than their parts, creating ecosystems that adapt, thrive, and enchant.

Envisioning a Multidimensional Universe

Imagine a brand as not just a name or a logo but as an expansive universe, where each digital platform is a realm. Websites, social media profiles, apps, and virtual worlds are not isolated entities; they are interconnected dimensions in the brand's galaxy. Each journey through this cosmos is an adventure, a seamless transition from one space to another, each platform a constellation in the brand's universe.

Reflect on brands like Nike, which have transcended their physical products to create a holistic experience. Engaging with their apps, participating in their community, wearing their products – every interaction is a step deeper into the Nike universe, where each experience enriches and extends the journey.

Contemplate Apple's ecosystem, a seamless tapestry where each device, each service, interweaves to create a unified narrative. The iPhone, the MacBook, the Apple Watch – each is a portal, an entry point into a broader Apple experience, transcending the physicality of devices to craft a continuous, immersive brand story.

In this new frontier of branding, we are not merely creating logos or slogans; we are building worlds. Worlds where customers do not just purchase products or services; they immerse themselves, live, and interact within the brand's universe. This is the zenith of branding – not just a strategy or a campaign, but the creation of experiences that are as limitless and boundless as the universe itself. Here, the brand becomes a cosmos, a space where imagination and reality converge, offering experiences that are not just consumed but lived and cherished.

User-Centric Approach: Empowering the Audience

Imagine a Dance of Collaboration

In the past, brands led the dance, dictating each step in their narrative. But times have changed, and now you're the lead. Think of brands as your dance partners—guiding, not dominating. This isn't a solo performance; it's a duet, a harmonious collaboration where your voice matters as much as theirs. Witness the transformation from a waltz to a tango—a dynamic shift that empowers and engages.

Brands as Choreographers, Not Conductors

Imagine the shift as a rebalancing act. Brands once conducted the orchestra, leading with authority. Now, they're more like choreographers—designing routines that showcase your strengths. Consider Dove's "Real Beauty" campaign—it's not just a product showcase; it's an invitation to step onto the dance floor and twirl to your rhythm. The brand isn't forcing a script; it's offering a stage for you to compose your story.

Empathy in Brand Relationships

Have you ever felt like a brand truly understands you? That's the magic of a user-centric approach. Brands no longer talk down to you; they lean in, listen, and hand you the microphone. Picture it as a shift from a solo act to a duet. You're not just a passive audience; you're a co-creator of the brand's story. This transformation isn't just about marketing; it's about democratizing brand narratives.

From Dictation to Collaboration

Gone are the days when brands solely dictated the narrative. We've entered an era where the audience isn't just a passive receiver; they're a co-author. Brands have relinquished creative control, giving customers the power to shape the story. It's a revolution where the brand's identity is co-forged by both creators and consumers.

Dove's Empowering Campaign

Dove's "Real Beauty" campaign is a perfect illustration of this shift. Instead of merely promoting soap, Dove sparked a movement challenging conventional beauty standards. They encouraged women to share unfiltered photos, celebrating their natural beauty. This user-centric approach elevated Dove's audience to become heroes of the brand story, empowering them to redefine beauty standards and forming an emotional connection beyond the product.

LEGO's Collaborative Platform

Consider LEGO's "LEGO Ideas" platform—a space not just for constructing sets, but for envisioning and sharing your designs. Enthusiasts propose new sets, vote on ideas, and see their creations become official LEGO products. LEGO's user-centric approach transforms enthusiasts into co-designers, injecting life into the brand's platform and nurturing a robust community.

You're the Artist of Your Story

Think of brands as canvases that invite you to pick up the brush. Imagine walking into an art gallery where each canvas holds a blank space, waiting for your creative strokes. LEGO's "LEGO Ideas" platform shifts you from spectator to artist; the brand isn't just a curator—it's a collaborator. The canvas isn't pre-filled; it's ready for you to leave your mark.

Collaborations and Co-Creation

A Grand Tapestry of Collaboration

Visualize a grand tapestry where threads from various sources are interwoven to create something truly beautiful. Brands are no longer isolated entities; they've become threads in this expansive tapestry. Collaboration isn't solely about expanding reach; it's about merging colors and textures to craft a more intricate whole. Brands that grasp the essence of this synergy tap into the innate human yearning for connection, igniting a resonance that goes beyond mere transactions.

A Symphony of Collaboration

Consider collaborations as a symphony, where each instrument contributes a distinct sound, yet together they orchestrate harmonious music. Brands, influencers, and customers collaborate akin to a seasoned ensemble, each bringing their unique expertise to create something that resonates on a deeper level. The collaboration between LEGO and NASA isn't confined to a mere set; it's a harmonious composition of expertise, bridging the gap between brick-building enthusiasts and real-life space explorers.

Ensemble Cast of Brands

Imagine brand collaborations as an ensemble cast in a compelling theater production. Just as actors complement one another's strengths to weave a captivating narrative, brands unite to tell an engaging story. Coca-Cola's "Freestyle" machines aren't merely dispensers; they're the players in a symphony, each offering a distinctive note that contributes to the overarching melody. The customer isn't just a passive audience member; they're an integral part of the cast, crafting their unique flavor story.

Fostering Community Through Collaboration

In this interconnected age, customers, influencers, and other brands blend harmoniously in a larger ensemble. Envision a symphony where these elements resonate, creating something greater than the sum of its parts. Collaborations are more than a means to extend reach; they foster a sense of community and shared purpose. Brands that embrace this synergy tap into the human desire for connection, invoking a resonance that transcends transactions.

Elevating Reach and Resonance

Through collaborations, whether with customers, influencers, or fellow brands, a brand's reach and resonance can soar to new heights. These partnerships go beyond transactional exchanges, nurturing a sense of community where shared values and creativity intertwine.

LEGO's Empowering Collaboration

LEGO's collaboration with NASA stands as a testament to the incredible power of collaboration. With the LEGO Ideas "Women of NASA" set, featuring mini figures of trailblazing women in space exploration, LEGO collaborated not only with their fan community but also with real-life space pioneers. This collaboration transformed their platform into a celebration of empowerment and education, unveiling the immense potential of co-creation.

Coca-Cola's Flavorful Collaboration

Consider Coca-Cola's "Freestyle" machines, allowing customers to craft their soda flavors. This transcends the simple act of choosing a beverage; it's about curating a personalized drink experience. Coca-Cola's platform transcends pre-packaged products; it encourages consumers to embark on an experiment, co-creating their own distinctive flavor combinations. The essence of collaboration lies with the customer, who becomes an active participant in the creative journey.

Digital Platforms and Brand Identity

Canvas of Brand Storytelling

Digital platforms aren't merely tools; they're expansive canvases for crafting brand narratives. A brand's social media profiles, websites, and apps are like rooms within a sprawling mansion, each revealing a distinct part of the story. Here, interactions cease to be one-way streets; they evolve into dynamic conversations that mold perceptions and foster connections.

Digital Palette of Brand Expression

Visualize a brand's digital presence as an awaiting palette of colors, ready to transform into a masterpiece. Every social media post, web page, and app screen is a brushstroke, adding texture and depth to the brand's narrative. This digital terrain isn't a mere landscape; it's a canvas where stories spring to life, a gallery where emotions are kindled, and an immersive realm where each click becomes a brushstroke that molds the brand's identity.

Symphony of Pixels and Code

Consider a brand's online presence akin to a symphony composed of pixels and code—a musical composition where notes blend seamlessly to craft a harmonious melody. The website transcends being a mere collection of pages; it transforms into a symphony of interactions, guiding users through an immersive journey. Social media profiles aren't static billboards; they are dynamic canvases that awaken with every scroll, enveloping users in the brand's visual and emotional narrative.

Digital Reflections of Identity

Imagine digital platforms as mirrors, reflecting not just appearances, but the very soul of a brand. Similar to how a mirror reveals more than mere reflections—it unveils character, emotions, and stories—brands' online presence unveils more than products; it reveals values, passions, and a profound connection with their audience. Red Bull's digital footprint transcends a mere assortment of videos; it acts as a mirror reflecting the spirit of adventure, inviting you to dive into a world of thrill and excitement.

Mosaic of Online Presence

The digital realm serves as a playground where brand stories come alive. Visualize a brand's online presence as a mosaic— an amalgamation of digital tiles, each contributing to a grander image. Social media, websites, and apps surpass the role of tools; they emerge as gateways that transport users deep into the core of a brand's narrative. By seamlessly intertwining these platforms, brands orchestrate a symphony of experiences mirroring the complexity of real life.

Red Bull's Adventure Identity

Red Bull's digital influence stretches far beyond energy drinks. Their YouTube channel boasts extreme sports content, music events, and astonishing stunts. By harnessing digital platforms, Red Bull has established a brand identity synonymous with adventure and adrenaline. Their content doesn't merely endorse energy drinks; it embodies a lifestyle and constructs a platform for enthusiasts of exhilarating experiences.

Marvel's Multifaceted Universe

Marvel Studios has elevated comic book heroes to global phenomena through their digital presence. Their interconnected universe isn't confined to movies alone; it extends across social media, games, merchandise, and even fan conventions. By embracing diverse digital platforms, Marvel furnishes fans with a multifaceted encounter that extends beyond screens, cultivating a unified brand identity cherished by millions.

Data-Driven Branding: Insights and Personalization

Data as the Brand's Compass

Data is far more than a collection of ones and zeros; it's the pulsating rhythm of a brand's strategy. It's the artist's palette that enriches the canvas of personalized brand experiences. It's the navigator that deciphers our audience's desires, often before they're articulated. Akin to a storyteller, data unveils the inclinations and dreams of the audience. Comparable to a GPS guiding a journey, data illuminates the path to sculpting tailor-made brand experiences. Yet, while data represents a trove of potential, it's imperative to proceed judiciously, balancing personalization with the reverence for privacy that each participant within this platform deserves. Like a guide, data must be employed ethically and responsibly, ensuring that the audience's privacy is preserved as they embark on this shared odyssey.

Data as the Brand's Guiding Stars

Envision data as a compass steering brands through the uncharted waters of consumer preferences. This isn't a mere assortment of digits; it's the blueprint of a customized expedition. Just as navigators once relied on stars to steer their course, brands utilize data points as their guiding constellations in the ocean of consumer desires. The compass doesn't dictate the journey; it illuminates the route, presenting insights into the unspoken yearnings of the audience.

Data as the Artist's Palette

Regard data as the artist's palette, where each data point is a vibrant hue awaiting fusion into a bespoke masterpiece. Brands aren't confined to crunching numbers; they're sculpting a symphony of personalization that resonates with individual predilections. Amazon's recommendation system isn't merely an algorithm; it functions as a conductor orchestrating a symphony of suggestions, leading you to unearth fresh gems based on your prior preferences.

Data as the Weaver of Personalization

Visualize data as a tapestry, interweaving individual strands of preference to craft a distinctive pattern for every consumer. Just as adept weavers merge diverse threads to forge intricate designs, brands interlace data points into a seamless tapestry of personalized encounters.

Amazon's Personal Shopper Approach

Amazon's recommendation system stands as a testament to data-driven personalization. When you explore Amazon, the platform proffers product suggestions founded on your browsing history and previous purchases. This data-fueled methodology refines your experience, rendering the shopping voyage more pertinent and pleasurable. Amazon's adeptness in wielding data converts its platform into a personal shopper, discerning your predilections even before you do.

Netflix's Intuitive Entertainment Curation

Netflix's recommendation algorithm constitutes the core of its personalization strategy. Netflix's recommendation algorithm isn't limited to a mere list of suggestions; it functions as an adept weaver fabricating a patchwork of entertainment that aligns with your interests and preferences. It beckons you to immerse yourself in a tailor-made viewing experience. When the platform proposes movies or shows rooted in your viewing history, it's not solely anticipatory; it's instinctual. Netflix harnesses data analytics to craft a portrayal of your predilections, curating a bespoke entertainment journey that feels akin to receiving whispered recommendations—enhancing the brand's bond with each user.

Measuring Success: Metrics

Metrics of Success

In this new epoch of branding, the benchmarks for success have evolved beyond mere sales figures to encompass something more intricate. Engagement, reach, and the resonance of user-generated content now serve as the new yardsticks of achievement. It's no longer solely about disseminating a message; it's about observing how far that message reverberates and resonates within the community you've nurtured.

Shifting the Definition of Success

The era when success was equated solely with sales figures has faded. In the realm of Brand-as-a-Platform, triumph manifests as the symphony of engagement, the echo of reach, and the choir of user-generated content. It transcends the act of selling; it's about striking chords that resonate. Metrics step forward as the scorecards that gauge the depth of connection a brand has cultivated with its audience—a mirror reflecting how adeptly the platform functions.

Resonating Success: A Symphony of Metrics

Envision brand success as a concert hall echoing with the applause of engaged and interconnected audiences. This isn't confined to sales statistics; it embraces the resonance of engagement, the harmonious expansion of reach, and the crescendo of user-generated content. Each metric surpasses being a mere numeral; it's a musical note within the symphony of brand-consumer relationships—an echo of how effectively the platform has struck harmonious chords with its audience.

Metrics as Parts in the Brand Story

Consider brand success metrics as parts within an unfolding narrative, akin to a book that chronicles the brand's influence. Just as each part builds upon the last, metrics construct a tale of engagement, reach, and affiliation. Starbucks' rewards program isn't merely about transactions; it weaves a tale of loyalty cultivated incrementally, crafting pages of commitment and belonging.

Metrics as Brushes on the Canvas of Loyalty

Envision metrics as brushes meticulously painting the portrait of brand loyalty, each stroke capturing an instance of engagement. Just as an artist overlays colors to create depth, brands layer metrics to portray a vibrant image of their relationship with the audience.

Nike's Active Interaction Canvas

Nike's "Nike Training Club" app is more than a tally of downloads; it's a canvas of interactions that immortalizes the involvement of active users embracing the brand's fitness narrative. It imbues depth and significance into the brand's canvas. This app illustrates how engagement metrics redefine triumph. It transcends the realm of mere downloads; it encapsulates the active users who immerse themselves in workouts and partake in the community. Nike's lens of success isn't confined to sales alone; it encompasses the impact on users' fitness journeys, nurturing relationships that transcend mere transactions.

Starbucks' Engagement Symphony

The Starbucks rewards program personifies engagement metrics. Increased engagement—ordering coffee, amassing stars, partaking in promotions—brings forth more rewards. Starbucks doesn't merely track transactions; they assess the degrees of engagement and interactions, crafting a platform that fosters a sense of belonging and an incentive for customers to return, all while savoring their preferred brew.

Challenges and Pitfalls: Navigating Brand Platform Complexity

Complexity in Building a Platform

The creation of a brand platform isn't devoid of challenges; it's akin to assembling a intricate puzzle composed of interlocking pieces. The pursuit of consistency across platforms, ensuring alignment of user-generated content with brand values, and managing the intricate web of interactions are obstacles that brands must adeptly navigate. It transforms into a continuous process of refinement, adaptation, and, at times, even reinvention.

Brand Platform: A Multilevel Mansion of Challenges

The act of constructing a brand platform mirrors the complexity of erecting a multi-story mansion. Every level introduces fresh challenges—sustaining coherence across platforms, navigating the labyrinthine realm of user-generated content, and preserving brand integrity amidst the multitude of voices. However, akin to architects, brands are tasked with confronting these challenges head-on, devising solutions that strike equilibrium between structure and adaptability, unity and diversity.

The Sea of Challenges in Brand Platform Navigation

Conceiving a brand platform resembles crafting a vessel to sail through uncharted waters. In much the same way a captain maneuvers turbulent seas, brands navigate the intricate expanse of brand platforms. It's not a mere puzzle awaiting resolution; it's a maze necessitating skilful navigation. Just as crafting a seaworthy vessel entails meticulous attention to detail—ranging from the durability of the hull to the precision of the sails—developing a brand platform requires astute consideration of factors like consistency, user-generated content, and brand fidelity.

Walking the Tightrope of Brand Platform Challenges

View the challenges of brand platforms as a delicate tightrope walk—a delicate equilibrium between brand identity and consumer empowerment. Similar to a tightrope walker's careful stride, brands balance between granting user autonomy and safeguarding brand values. The "Share a Coke" campaign by Coca-Cola illustrates this challenge by exemplifying the need for precision in balancing personalization and inclusivity. It underscores the notion that even well-intended platforms necessitate meticulous equilibrium.

Crafting a Mosaic of Complexity in Brand Platforms

Consider the process of crafting a brand platform as akin to assembling a mosaic—where each piece is distinctive yet contributes to the broader panorama. Similar to a mosaic artist who meticulously selects each tile, brands must cautiously determine how user-generated content blends into the fabric of the platform's narrative. The case of McDonald's "Create Your Taste" platform highlights the complexity associated with incorporating user-generated content seamlessly. It serves as a reminder that even influential entities can encounter challenges when attempting to harmonize diverse elements.

Balancing Act: Coca-Cola's Experience with "Share a Coke"

Coca-Cola's "Share a Coke" campaign encountered challenges when personalizing bottles with individual names. While the concept was heart-warming, controversies arose due to omitted or misspelled names. Coca-Cola navigated this complexity by embracing feedback and refining their approach, highlighting that even well-intentioned platforms can falter without careful management.

Navigating Complexity: McDonald's "Create Your Taste"

Even industry titans like McDonald's can face platform challenges. Their "Create Your Taste" initiative aimed to offer customized burger options. However, the intricacy of the platform led to operational issues and confusion for both customers and employees. This example underscores that even with honorable intentions, platforms can stumble if simplicity and user-friendliness aren't central to their design.

Future Trends: The Evolution of Brand Platforms

Technology's Creative Brushstrokes on Brand-as-a-Platform

The future isn't a distant horizon; it's being woven into the very fabric of the present. Emerging technologies such as augmented reality, virtual reality, and artificial intelligence are akin to masterful brushstrokes on the canvas of Brand-as-a-Platform. These technologies are the ingredients that flavor tomorrow's interactions, painting a vivid picture of a future where brand experiences are even more immersive, interactive, and awe-inspiring.

The Future Canvas: Technology's Creative Magic

Peer into the future, and you'll catch glimpses of a reality where brand platforms are illuminated by the magic of technology. Envision a world where virtual reality effortlessly transports you to immersive brand realms or where artificial intelligence adeptly tailors experiences to your individual preferences. These forthcoming trends aren't distant fables; they're the innovative brushstrokes that will shape the landscapes of tomorrow—a testament to the perpetual evolution of Brand-as-a-Platform.

Threads of the Future: Technology's Impact on Brand Platforms

Imagine a tapestry woven from threads of the future—augmented reality, virtual reality, and artificial intelligence adding depth and texture to the fabric of Brand-as-a-Platform. This isn't a far-off dream; it's a canvas already being painted with strokes of innovation. Envision a realm where brand experiences seamlessly transcend the confines of screens, where immersion and interaction ascend to unprecedented heights, all thanks to the imaginative strokes of technology.

Future as an Unwritten Story: Technology's Plot Twists

Poder the future of brand platforms as a tale yet to be penned, with each emerging technology serving as a plot twist that enthralls readers. In much the same way a skilled storyteller crafts anticipation with every turn of the page, brands cultivate anticipation with each integration of cutting-edge technology. Take IKEA's "Place" app as a preview of what lies ahead, where augmented reality transforms furniture shopping into a visual adventure, bridging the gap between imagination and reality.

Brand Platform's Future Garden: Seeds of Innovation

Imagine the future of brand platforms as a lush garden where seeds of innovation are being sown. With time, each seed blooms into an experience that captures the essence of tomorrow. Consider Amazon's Alexa not just as an artificial intelligence assistant, but as a futuristic companion that presciently tends to your needs. This AI-driven presence acts like a gardener nurturing your requests, transforming the platform into more than just a solution provider—into a partner that surprises you with solutions you might not have even conceived of.

Glimpse of the Future: IKEA's "Place" App

Take IKEA's "Place" app as a glimpse into the future. By utilizing augmented reality, this app enables users to visualize how IKEA furniture would appear in their homes prior to purchase. This innovative approach doesn't merely elevate the shopping experience; it morphs IKEA's platform into a tool for informed decision-making, seamlessly integrating the brand into the daily lives of customers.

Future Companion: Amazon's Alexa

The trajectory of brand platforms is embodied in Amazon's Alexa. This isn't solely about voice-activated devices; it's about creating an AI-powered assistant that harmoniously assimilates into users' lives. Amazon's platform transcends product sales, evolving into a responsive presence that not only fulfills users' needs—whether that entails weather updates or grocery orders—but also delights them with solutions that exceed their expectations. This AI-driven evolution imparts a sense of indispensability to the platform, transforming it into an indispensable companion on the brand journey.

Emotional Resonance: Connecting Beyond Transactions

Brands as Old Friends: Heartfelt Connections

Visualize brands as familiar companions you've known for years. This isn't merely a business transaction; it's a profound and heartfelt connection. Just as old friends share both laughter and tears, brands share in the journey of your life, seamlessly becoming a part of your story. Think of brands as steadfast companions on your life's path, transcending their role as mere products. This connection is akin to a warm embrace—a comforting presence that lingers long after the interaction concludes.

Symphony of Emotions: Brand Resonance

Imagine brand resonance as a symphony of emotions, with each note echoing a sentiment that reverberates deep within. Just as a masterfully composed melody stirs your soul, brands evoke emotions that transcend rationality. Reflect upon the emotional resonance that brands like Apple or Disney elicit— an overwhelming sense of belonging, a connection to something greater than oneself, and a feeling of identity woven through shared values and collective experiences.

Shared Journey's Heartbeats: Brands as Companions

Envision this emotional bond as the rhythmic heartbeats of a shared journey. Brands are more than mere labels; they become fellow travelers in the narrative of your life. Just as fellow travelers shape the essence of a journey, brands shape the narrative of your life's journey. Contemplate the personal anecdotes of individuals who cherish a profound connection with brands like Starbucks. These individuals share stories of how a simple coffee shop has transformed into a backdrop for cherished moments, meaningful conversations, and deep personal reflections.

Brand Empowerment: Beyond Athletic Wear

Consider the brand Nike—a symbol that transcends selling athletic wear to stand for empowerment and perseverance. When you don a Nike product, it's not merely a logo you're wearing; you're embodying a mindset. This emotional connection serves as a bridge, linking you to a global community of athletes who resonate with the same values. Through impactful campaigns and compelling advertisements, Nike has evolved from a sportswear entity into an emblem of determination, motivating individuals to shatter their own boundaries.

As you embark on this transformative journey of Brand-as-a-Platform, the emotional resonance between brands and individuals emerges as a defining element, underlining the depth of connection that goes beyond transactional interactions. This bond is a testament to the enduring power of brands to become companions, confidants, and sources of inspiration in our lives.

Ethical Dimensions: Walking the Tightrope of Responsibility

Stages of Ethical Values: Pushing Boundaries Responsibly

Visualize brand platforms as stages where ethical values are both tested and showcased. This goes beyond mere boundary-pushing; it's about doing so with a strong sense of responsibility. Just as a trapeze artist skillfully balances grace and daring, brands must adeptly navigate the fine line between innovation and ethical considerations. Imagine ethical principles as the tightrope wire—requiring a delicate equilibrium between captivating performances and the practice of responsible conduct.

Guiding Compass of Ethics: Navigating Uncharted Territories

Consider the ethical dimensions of brand platforms as the compass guiding brands through unexplored territories. Just as historical explorers were guided by their unwavering principles and values, modern brands navigate intricate landscapes with a keen awareness of audience sensitivities and societal norms. Reflect on exemplary cases such as Patagonia, a brand that staunchly advocates for environmental responsibility. Such cases demonstrate how a brand's platform can serve as a potent instrument for promoting positive change while respecting ethical considerations.

Cornerstone of Ethical Responsibility: Building on Solid Foundations

Imagine ethical responsibility as a foundational cornerstone that supports the weight of brand platforms. Just as an architect ensures the solidity of a foundation before designing a magnificent structure, brands must ensure that their platforms are constructed upon unwavering ethical principles. Reflect on instances where brands faced and surmounted ethical dilemmas, showcasing that navigating the tightrope of responsibility requires constant vigilance, adaptability, and an unyielding commitment to doing what's right.

Ethical Challenge: Everlane's Transparent Journey

Consider the ethical challenge encountered by the clothing brand Everlane—an enterprise known for its transparent pricing and dedication to sustainability. When introducing a new line, Everlane openly shared the hurdles it confronted in terms of supply chain transparency and ethical production. This candid approach deeply resonated with its audience, illustrating how brands can effectively navigate ethical complexities by being transparent about their journey and trials. This transparency lends a profound depth to their platform, demonstrating that ethical responsibility is not a mere slogan but an integral facet of their brand identity.

As brands stride upon the platform of Brand-as-a-Platform, they are entrusted with the responsibility to not just captivate but to uphold ethical values that resonate with their audience. This part underscores the critical importance of balancing innovation with responsibility, presenting ethical dimensions as both challenges and opportunities for brands to elevate their platforms while fostering a positive impact on individuals and society.

Cultural Immersion: Brand Platforms and Global Identity

Brands as Bridges: Connecting Cultures Across Continents

Envision brand platforms as bridges that transcend geographical boundaries, forging connections between cultures and spanning continents. Brands are not restricted by borders; they are global storytellers with the power to transcend space. Just as intrepid travelers return with tales from distant lands, brand platforms bring diverse narratives to your fingertips. Consider brand platforms as portals that effortlessly transport you to different cultures—gateways that transcend languages and obstacles, offering a digital passport to understanding and fostering connection.

Cultural Ambassadors of Brand Platforms: Sharing Stories Beyond Commerce

Reflect on the profound impact of brand platforms as cultural ambassadors, serving as conduits for stories that extend far beyond commerce. Just as a diplomatic ambassador nurtures relations between nations, brands cultivate connections by sharing the very essence of various cultures. Contemplate the role of platforms such as YouTube, where content creators from all corners of the globe share their perspectives. This exchange of narratives dismantles cultural barriers and champions global comprehension.

Cultural Tapestry of Brand Platforms: Interweaving Threads of Diversity

Imagine cultural immersion as a tapestry adorned with threads woven from different cultures. Just as a tapestry displays the artistry of diverse regions, brand platforms mirror the multiplicity of global narratives. Consider the anecdotes of individuals who have connected with brands from distinct cultures, sharing how these interactions have broadened their horizons. These encounters enrich their lives through shared experiences and cross-cultural learning, illuminating the potential of brand platforms to bridge cultures.

Airbnb's Cultural Bridge: Beyond Accommodation to Authentic Experiences

Contemplate the case of Airbnb—a platform not solely focused on accommodations but dedicated to immersing travelers in local culture. When you book a stay through Airbnb, you're not merely securing a place to rest; you're gaining access to authentic experiences deeply rooted in the host's culture and lifestyle. Through this innovative platform, Airbnb forges connections that traverse geographical barriers. It provides a window into the lives of individuals hailing from different cultures, effectively transforming into a bridge that spans continents. This bridge fosters connections by sharing stories and experiences that traverse borders, affirming the power of brand platforms in championing global unity.

As brands step onto the global stage of Brand-as-a-Platform, they evolve into more than just commercial entities. They become vehicles that facilitate cross-cultural interaction, engendering understanding, and offering a platform for shared experiences. This segment underscores the significance of brand platforms as instruments of cultural exchange, showcasing their role in transcending geographical boundaries and building bridges that amplify our collective human story.

The Brand Platform Blueprint

The following mental model can serve as a strategic guide, offering you a blueprint to understand, create, and optimize their brand platforms. Just as a blueprint provides a plan for constructing a building, "The Brand Platform Blueprint" offers a structured approach to building and navigating the dynamic world of Brand-as-a-Platform.

1. **The Platform Parable:** View your brand as a dynamic platform that invites engagement and co-creation. Imagine stepping onto this stage where customers become active participants in your brand's story, transcending traditional transactions for a more immersive experience.

2. **Brand Seasons of Transformation:** Visualize your brand's evolution like the changing of seasons. Just as nature adapts to rhythms, brands shift from selling products to curating resonant stories. Embrace this transformational journey to connect with changing consumer expectations.

3. **Ecosystem Harmony:** Envision your brand's touchpoints as interconnected spaces in a grand ballroom. Cultivate a seamless and immersive ecosystem where customers can journey through different dimensions of your brand's universe, ensuring a cohesive and unforgettable experience.

4. **Dialogues, Not Monologues:** Imagine your brand narrative as a harmonious duet. Transition from dictating to dialoguing with your audience. Just as two voices come together, collaborate with customers to co-author stories that reflect shared values and aspirations.

5. **Symphony of Collaboration:** Picture your brand collaborations as an orchestra. Align with customers, influencers, and other brands to create a symphony of voices that foster community and purpose. Just as diverse instruments harmonize, partnerships amplify resonance and reach.

6. **Digital Canvases of Identity:** Think of digital platforms as rooms in a mansion, each contributing to your brand's larger narrative. Utilize online profiles, websites, and apps as canvases to paint the rich tapestry of your brand's experiences and identity.

7. **Data Compass:** Use data insights as your guiding compass. Similar to a GPS, data illuminates the path to understanding customer preferences, enabling personalized experiences while respecting privacy boundaries.

8. **Resonance Scorecard:** View success metrics as a symphony's scorecard. Measure engagement, reach, and resonance to gauge the depth of connection with your audience. Just as music resonates, these metrics reflect your brand platform's impact.

9. **Adaptive Architect:** Approach your brand platform like an evolving structure. Think of an architect refining designs. Balance structure with flexibility, addressing challenges while maintaining your brand's core integrity and adaptability.

10. **Innovation Palette:** Visualize emerging technologies as artistic tools. Just as brushstrokes shape a canvas, use augmented reality, virtual reality, and AI to paint the next part of brand experiences, creating immersive and remarkable interactions.

11. **Emotive Companionship:** Think of your brand as an old friend. Cultivate emotional connections that go beyond transactions, becoming companions on your customer's

journey. Create lasting memories and a sense of identity through shared experiences.

12. **Ethical Tightrope:** Imagine ethical decisions as a tightrope walk. Balance innovation with integrity, much like a trapeze artist balances grace and daring. Maintain transparency and responsible practices to enhance your platform's impact and credibility.

13. **Cultural Bridges:** Visualize your brand as a bridge between cultures. Just as travelers connect with diverse communities, your platform can bridge cultural gaps, fostering connections and understanding through authentic narratives.

The above mental model encapsulates the core concepts of each section in this part, providing you with a tangible framework to navigate the intricate landscape of Brand-as-a-Platform.

Insights in Numbers: Illuminating Branding Trends

1. According to a study by **Deloitte,** 90% of consumers want brands to actively engage in societal issues, showing the increasing importance of values and purpose in branding.

2. **HubSpot** reports that 54% of consumers want more video content from brands they support, highlighting the growing demand for engaging visual content.

3. **Adobe's State of Content Report** states that 68% of consumers prefer to learn about a product or brand through content, indicating the significance of informative and engaging brand platforms.

4. In a survey by **Stackla**, 86% of consumers believe authenticity is a key factor in decidingwhich brands they support, emphasizing the importance of genuine and relatable brand narratives.

5. According to **IBM**, 81% of CEOs believe that technology is the single most important external factor shaping organizations today, underscoring the role of technology in the evolution of brand platforms.

6. **Edelman's Trust Barometer** reveals that 81% of consumers say that trust is a deal-breaker when considering a purchase from a new brand, highlighting the role of trust in building successful brand platforms.

7. In a study by **Content Marketing Institute**, 90% of top-performing B2B content marketers put their audience's needs ahead of their company's promotional message, emphasizing the user-centric approach.

8. According to **Smart Insights**, 49% of organizations do not have a defined digital marketing strategy, indicating the need for brands to strategically design their digital brand platforms.

9. In a **PwC survey**, 59% of consumers surveyed said that companies need to actively share their values, showing the desire for brands to engage on a deeper level beyond just products.

10. **Statista** predicts that by 2025, the number of worldwide social media users is expected to reach around 4.41 billion, further highlighting the significance of digital platforms for brand engagement.

Brand Audit Exercises: Crafting Your Brand Platform Strategy

Imagine stepping into the shoes of a brand archaeologist, armed with a magnifying glass and a sense of adventure. As we venture further into the captivating realm of Brand-as-a-Platform, consider this part your expedition—a guided exploration into the heart of your brand's identity and potential.

Now, let's introduce you to some insightful companions on this journey. Meet Laura, our branding sage. With a cup of steaming tea in hand, Laura leans in and imparts her wisdom, "Think of your brand platform as the heartbeat of your business—a rhythmic dance between your values and your customers' aspirations. It's where connections flourish and stories are co-authored."

And amidst the exploration, humor steps in as your travel buddy. Imagine the witty remarks of Mark, a seasoned comedian, adding a playful touch to your quest. "Building a brand is like cooking," Mark chuckles, "A dash of authenticity, a pinch of relatability, and a whole lot of 'yum' factor. Your platform is where the feast of your brand story unfolds—so make sure it's a tantalizing experience!"

As you embark on these Brand Audit Exercises, envision yourself as a conductor orchestrating a symphony of brand elements. It's not just about analyzing; it's about weaving together a tapestry that resonates, engages, and speaks volumes to your audience.

With Laura's insightful guidance and Mark's humorous quips by your side, these exercises become more than a mere checklist—they become a journey of self-discovery and creative exploration. Imagine the thrill of unearthing hidden gems within your brand and crafting a platform that's not just captivating but also authentic.

So, dear explorer, with expert insights and humor as your compass, let's delve into these Brand Audit Exercises. Together, let's reveal the layers, unveil the potential, and transform your brand into a resonant platform that leaves a lasting imprint.

Ready? Let's embark on this expedition of transformation— one where your brand's story is waiting to be uncovered and shared with the world. It's time to paint a masterpiece, curate an experience, and create a space where your audience becomes part of the story. Your journey starts now.

Brand Identity Reflection:

Take a moment to reflect on your brand's identity. What adjectives or emotions would you use to describe your brand? How does your brand resonate with your target audience? Compare this with how you want your brand to be perceived. Identify any gaps and consider how your brand platform can bridge them.

Customer Journey Mapping:

Map out your customer's journey from awareness to engagement and beyond. Where do they interact with your brand? How do these touchpoints contribute to the overall brand experience? Identify areas where you can enhance engagement, encourage co-creation, or foster community-building.

Interactive Content Ideation:

Brainstorm ideas for interactive content that can transform your brand's online presence. What types of interactive experiences can you offer to engage your audience on digital platforms? Consider quizzes, polls, virtual events, and challenges that invite participation.

Collaboration Exploration:

Explore potential collaboration opportunities for your brand. Identify influencers, organizations, or complementary brands that align with your values and goals. How can these collaborations amplify your platform and create a shared narrative?

User-Centric Analysis:

Analyze your brand's interactions from a user-centric perspective. How well are you listening to your customers? How can you shift from a monologue to a dialogue with your audience? Brainstorm ways to empower your customers to become co-creators of your brand's story.

Data-Driven Insights:

Examine the data you have about your customers' preferences and behaviors. How can you leverage this data to offer more personalized experiences? Explore ways to use data insights to enhance engagement and tailor your brand platform to individual preferences.

Platform Resonance Assessment:

Assess how resonant your brand platform is with your target audience. What emotions or associations does your brand evoke? Are there any disconnects between your desired platform and how it's perceived? Consider how you can align your platform more closely with your audience's aspirations.

Innovation Brainstorming:

Imagine how emerging technologies can enhance your brand platform. How can augmented reality, virtual reality, or AI elevate your brand's interactions? Brainstorm creative ways to incorporate these technologies to create more immersive and engaging experiences.

Ethical Considerations Dialogue:

Engage in a dialogue about the ethical considerations of your brand platform. How can you ensure responsible data usage and protect user privacy? Reflect on your brand's values and how they guide your platform's practices.

Storytelling Alignment:

Analyze the stories your brand tells and how they align with the platform's goals. Do these stories reflect the collaborative and immersive nature of your platform? Consider how you can tell stories that emphasize community, empowerment, and shared experiences.

Shaping the Future of Branding

As we draw the curtains on this immersive exploration of Brand-as-a-Platform, it's evident that we've embarked on a journey that transcends the conventional confines of branding. Our voyage through the parts has revealed a landscape where brands evolve into living ecosystems, where interactions are symphonies, and where consumers are co-creators of narratives.

Just as a masterful orchestra harmonizes diverse instruments to create a symphony that resonates, a brand platform orchestrates its elements—values, experiences, narratives, and interactions—to compose an unforgettable melody that reverberates with its audience. This symphony isn't merely played for the masses; it's co-authored with them, reflecting their desires, aspirations, and individuality.

Our exploration has shown that in a world where consumer expectations are evolving and technology is advancing at a rapid pace, the transformation from traditional branding to a resonant brand platform is not just a choice; it's an imperative. The lessons from legacy brands that have transformed themselves into living platforms—where customers co-author stories, where interactions transcend transactions, and where authenticity is a guiding light—reinforce the notion that the future belongs to those who dare to stand out.

As we close this part, remember that your brand has the power to be a beacon of innovation, a canvas of co-creation, and a stage for shared experiences. Whether you're a seasoned marketer, an entrepreneur, or simply someone curious about the evolving landscape of branding, you now hold the blueprint to forge connections that go beyond the transactional, to craft stories that resonate, and to transform your brand into an ever-evolving platform.

Just as the final note of a melody lingers in the air, may the insights, anecdotes, and exercises you've encountered here linger in your mind. Carry them with you as you venture into the dynamic world of branding, armed with the understanding that your brand isn't just a product or service—it's a platform, a stage, and an invitation for your audience to step into an unfolding story.

So, embrace the transformation, wield the power of technology with purpose, and let your brand resonate with authenticity. The symphony of Brand-as-a-Platform is yours to compose, and its resonance will echo through the hearts and minds of those who join you on this remarkable journey.

As you step into the future of branding, may your brand's platform be a stage that sparks connections, cultivates relationships, and leaves an indelible mark in the ever-evolving narrative of our world.

Thank you for joining us on this exploration. Your journey continues, and your brand's platform is ready to take center stage.

Reflections

Products to Platforms

Step	Description	Example	Key Takeaways/ Strategies	Challenges/ Considerations
1	**Start Strong**	Develop a robust product with a substantial user base. Example: Adobe's Creative Cloud Suite, including Photoshop and Illustrator, serves as a strong starting product.	- Ensure product defensibility - Attract a critical mass of users	- Identifying the right product-market fit - Competition in the product space
2	**Embrace Hybrid Model**	Combine product and platform strategies. Example: Adobe transitioned from selling standalone software products to offering a subscription-based Creative Cloud platform, providing continuous updates and cloud-based collaboration.	- Identify opportunities for value creation - Balance product and platform focus	- Managing the transition from product to platform mindset - Ensuring compatibility with third-party offerings

Step	Description	Example	Key Takeaways/ Strategies	Challenges/ Considerations
3	**Drive User Conversion**	Facilitate user migration with compelling value. Example: Adobe incentivized users to switch to Creative Cloud by offering cloud storage, regular software updates, and access to a broader creative ecosystem.	- Create sufficient new value - Stay consistent with your brand - Involve users in improvements	- Overcoming user inertia to shift to the platform - Ensuring consistent quality and safety standards for third-party offerings
4	**Deter Imitation**	Safeguard against competitors through control and innovation. Example: Adobe maintains control over its proprietary file formats and integrates its tools with other popular software, making it difficult for competitors to replicate its ecosystem.	- Identify openings for value creation - Control proprietary aspects - Consider exclusivity agreements	- Monitoring the competitive landscape for imitators - Balancing openness with proprietary control

Power of Platforms

Key Concepts and Shifts	Description
Background	In 2007, mobile-phone industry leaders were Nokia, Samsung, etc. The iPhone disrupted this status quo.
iPhone's Dominance	By 2015, the iPhone commanded 92% of global profits, while former leaders struggled to stay profitable.
Strategic Advantages	Incumbents had product differentiation, trusted brands, tech, but lost to iPhone.
Power of Platforms	Apple used a platform connecting developers and users, generating value through network effects.
Transition Shifts	Moving from a traditional pipeline to a platform involves shifts in resource control, external interaction, and ecosystem value.
Forces Within Ecosystem	Platform participants can contribute or compete, demanding effective governance.
Forces by Ecosystem	Platforms can disrupt unrelated industries, reshaping competitors' landscapes.
Shift in Focus	Traditional firms focus on sales; platforms prioritize interactions, core exchanges, and network effects.
Access and Governance	Decisions about access and governance encourage value creation and prevent exploitation.
Metrics	Platforms rely on metrics like interaction success, engagement, match quality, and mitigating negative network effects.
Financial Value	Platforms gauge the financial value of their communities and network effects, defying conventional metrics.
Leadership Style	Platform leadership requires an external orientation, ecosystem nurturing, and value creation, differing from top-down management.
Challenges for Pipelines	Traditional pipeline businesses must adapt to new strategic rules or face obsolescence.

Key considerations for building a successful platform

Key Consideration	Description	Insights and Tips
Rapid User Acquisition	Quickly gain a critical mass of users by leveraging existing platforms or public data.	- Build a referral program to encourage user-generated growth. - Utilize social media advertising and targeted marketing campaigns. - Consider partnerships or collaborations to access complementary user bases.
Stand-Alone Value	Ensure your platform offers unique value to individual users, even without a large user base.	- Continuously gather and analyze user feedback to enhance user experience. - Invest in user education and tutorials to showcase the platform's capabilities. - Address pain points and provide solutions tailored to your target audience.
Building Credibility	Attract reputable partners or contributors to enhance trust and reputation in a competitive market.	- Establish thought leadership through content creation and industry insights. - Seek endorsements or testimonials from satisfied users. - Highlight any industry awards, certifications, or partnerships that showcase your credibility.
Effective Pricing Strategies	Implement strategic pricing models like pay-as-you-go and user subsidies to attract and retain users.	- Offer flexible pricing plans to accommodate different user needs and budgets. - Monitor market trends and adjust pricing strategies accordingly. - Use data analytics to identify pricing optimization opportunities.

Key Consideration	Description	Insights and Tips
Compatibility with Existing Systems	Strive for seamless integration with legacy systems, making the transition smoother and highlighting the platform's advantages.	- Conduct extensive testing and quality assurance to ensure compatibility with widely used legacy systems. - Provide comprehensive migration guides and support to assist users during the transition process. - Highlight the benefits and efficiencies gained by using your platform in tandem with existing systems.

MACE as a Blueprint

MACE Framework Component	Description	Strategies and Insights
Mastery	Reward user engagement with unique, non-transferrable incentives.	- Foster public displays of affinity and small sacrifices. - Constantly innovate to deliver distinctive value. - Example: Hasbro's Magic brandwith innovative products like Secret Lair.
Accessibility	Maximize brand accessibility through pricing, distribution, and appeal strategies.	- Offer cost-effective entry-level products or free options. - Leverage alternative pricing models. - Utilize diverse sales channels. - Appeal to various customer demographics. - Example: Marvel's films with broad appeal.

MACE Framework Component	Description	Strategies and Insights
Cadence	Maintain brand relevance with a continuous flow of content and product updates.	- Regularly release new products or updates. - Transform long-form content into micro-content. - Encourage user-generated contributions. - Embrace transparency, even in times of failure. - Example: Apple's response to the Taylor Swift controversy.
Ensnarement	Enhance brand stickiness through switching costs and network effects.	- Establish systemized product lines over one-off releases. - Incorporate features encouraging user interaction and sharing. - Harness user data to optimize algorithms. - Example: LEGO's product line strategy and Coca-Cola's Share-A-Coke campaign.

Why Customers Leave Platforms

Factors Contributing to Disintermediation	Strategies to Prevent Disintermediation
Urgency: The need to solve a problem now.	- Provide quick solutions for urgent needs. - Offer on-demand services.
Rake: The platform charge for facilitating a deal.	- Lower transaction fees. - Shift monetization to where the platform adds the most value.

Factors Contributing to Disintermediation	Strategies to Prevent Disintermediation
Risk: The danger that a deal will go badly.	- Offer reputation systems, insurance, and mediation services. - Enhance safety measures. - Provide guarantees and insurance options.
Skill: The level of expertise required for the task.	- Focus on value addition for high-skill tasks. - Build trust and reputation systems.
Interaction Frequency: How often partners must communicate.	- Design carrots and incentives for continuous on-platform interactions. - Implement rewards and loyalty programs.
Project Modularity: The degree tasks can be divided into smaller components.	- Create value for both the first and subsequent interactions. - Develop features that encourage multi-stage or modular projects on the platform. - Utilize automated tracking and billing for ongoing projects.

Transforming Products into Platform

Demand-Side Evolution Steps	Supply-Side Evolution Steps	Examples
1. Structuring a love group	- Internal product R&D + external complementors	- Makerbot: Attracting product fans among the maker community.
2. Transforming love group into early adopters	- Internal platform R&D + blended complementors + community management	- GoPro: Engaging extreme sports enthusiasts through marketing and community events.

Demand-Side Evolution Steps	Supply-Side Evolution Steps	Examples
3. Leveraging early adopters to accelerate platform adoption	Hybrid business model management	- Lego: Opening code for Mindstorm robots to create a platform. - Nest: Actively working with external companies to develop Nest-compatible products.
4. Establishing a sustainable ecosystem	- Foster continuous innovation and user engagement - Encourage community-driven development and feedback - Implement strategies for long-term platform growth and sustainability	- Apple: Creating a vibrant ecosystem around iOS, with continuous updates and a strong app developer community. - Amazon: Developing a vast marketplace with varied sellers and continuous expansion.

PART-2

REVENUE SUBSCRIBED

SECURING SUSTAINABLE SUCCESS

Securing Sustainable Success

In the harmonious tapestry of business evolution, where brands morph into platforms, a new symphony emerges — the symphony of subscription triumphs. Building upon the foundation laid in the previous part, where we explored how brands can transcend traditional roles and become platforms for diverse offerings, we now delve deeper into the symphonic narratives of enterprises that have mastered the art of subscriptions.

As the crescendo of brand-as-a-platform thinking echoes through these subscription success stories, we witness how businesses have amplified their resonance by embracing subscription models. Just as a platform beckons various participants, subscriptions orchestrate an engagement symphony that unites businesses and consumers in an ongoing partnership. In this part, we explore how this partnership has evolved into symphonies of value, engagement, and loyalty.

From the platforms that fostered diverse ecosystems, we transition to the platforms that have harmonized with subscription dynamics. These platforms, rather than being static landscapes, have become dynamic stages where customers and brands engage in an ever-evolving dance of value exchange. These stories exemplify how platforms, when interwoven with subscription models, can create a new kind of harmony in the business-consumer relationship.

Much like a musical score building upon recurring motifs, this part builds upon the notion that businesses are evolving beyond transactional exchanges. The stage is set for subscription models to be the underlying rhythm that sustains these evolving platforms.

We'll journey through diverse industries, each movement revealing how businesses have dared to venture into the realm of subscription offerings, transforming industries and resonating deeply with subscribers.

Join us as we explore the evolution from brands as platforms to brands as platforms with symphonic subscription dynamics. In doing so, we'll uncover not only the tales of subscription triumphs but also the harmonies that these businesses have composed with their audiences. Let's delve into the orchestration of subscription offerings and how they play a pivotal role in amplifying the resonance of brand-as-a-platform strategies.

In a realm where business strategies clash and evolve, one paradigm has risen to prominence, reshaping revenue generation as we know it: the Subscription Model. Buckle up as we delve deep into this realm of recurrent possibilities, exploring the nuances of advantage, the labyrinth of challenge, and the compass guiding triumphant subscription implementations.

Decoding the Elixir:
The Subscription Model Unveiled

Step into the realm where customers aren't just buyers; they're members of an exclusive club. The Subscription Model, a masterstroke of commerce, is the key that opens doors to recurring revenue streams. A symphony of customized offerings, from streaming epics to curated culinary journeys, it's the promise of convenience, tailored perfectly to customer cravings.

Dive into the transformative world of the Subscription Model, an innovative paradigm shift in the realm of modern commerce. This approach transcends the conventional transactional relationship between businesses and customers, fostering a dynamic where purchasers are not merely buyers but cherished members of a distinguished club. This model is a beacon of ingenuity in the marketplace, unlocking the potential for consistent and predictable revenue streams, a coveted goal for any business.

The essence of the Subscription Model lies in its ability to turn ordinary transactions into an extraordinary journey of continual engagement and personalized experiences. It's a world where customers don't just buy products; they subscribe to an ethos, a lifestyle. From the enthralling escapades of streaming services to the gastronomic adventures offered by curated food subscriptions, this model is a celebration of bespoke convenience, crafted to align seamlessly with the evolving desires and needs of the consumer.

What sets this model apart is its emphasis on customization and exclusivity. Every aspect of the service or product is fine-tuned to resonate with the individual tastes and preferences of subscribers, offering them a sense of ownership and personalization. It's a harmonious blend of utility and pleasure, where the convenience of having essentials delivered meshes with the joy of discovering new favorites in each package.

Moreover, the Subscription Model nurtures a community-centric ethos. Subscribers are not isolated consumers; they are part of a vibrant community, sharing experiences and growing together. This sense of belonging strengthens the bond between the brand and its customers, transforming routine purchases into a part of the subscribers' identity and daily life.

In this dynamic and ever-evolving market, the Subscription Model stands as a testament to innovation in customer engagement. It offers a narrative where customers are active participants, not passive consumers. This model isn't just a mechanism for steady revenue; it's a forward-thinking approach to building lasting relationships with customers, inviting them to embark on a journey of discovery, convenience, and unparalleled personalization.

Dancing with Benefits: Symphony of Subscription Gains

Harmony of Predictability: The Steady Cadence of Revenue

Imagine a world where revenue isn't a turbulent tide but a gentle, steady river. With subscriptions, you're not riding the unpredictable waves of one-time purchases; you're sailing with a tranquil predictability. Each subscription payment that flows in becomes a note in a symphony of financial stability. This harmony allows for more accurate forecasting and strategic planning, letting you navigate the business landscape with confidence.

Take, for instance, Adobe's shift to the subscription model with Adobe Creative Cloud. Rather than relying solely on sporadic software purchases, they embraced subscriptions, ensuring a consistent flow of revenue. This harmony allows them to plan long-term projects, invest in innovation, and maintain a more resilient business model.

Tango of Loyalty: From Customers to Aficionados

Subscribers aren't just customers; they're enthusiasts, devotees who've pledged their loyalty. The Subscription Model has an enchanting power to transform mere clients into ardent aficionados. This transformation is the heartbeat of subscription success. With every renewal, your subscribers reaffirm their faith in your brand, becoming the bedrock upon which your business stands. The tango of loyalty is a dance that nurtures relationships beyond transactions, creating a community that champions your offerings.

Consider Amazon Prime, which transformed its subscribers into loyalists. Beyond its renowned shipping perks, Amazon bundled services like Prime Video and Kindle Unlimited into the subscription. This tango of loyalty fostered a community of devoted members who remain engaged, spread brand advocacy, and significantly contributed to Amazon's growth across various verticals.

Whispers of Data: Unveiling Consumer Desires

In the heart of subscriptions lies a treasure trove of insights. Every interaction, every choice a subscriber makes, whispers their desires to you. Subscriptions illuminate the path to understanding your customers on an intimate level. From consumption patterns to preferences, these insights paint vivid portraits of consumer desires. It's not just about what they're purchasing; it's about why. The whispers of data enable you to fine-tune your offerings, creating experiences that resonate deeply.

Netflix, for example, leverages data to analyze viewership patterns, helping them tailor content recommendations and produce original shows that align with viewer preferences. Through the whispers of data, they've managed to predict audience trends, curate personalized content, and even optimize marketing strategies to attract new subscribers.

Climb to Crescendo: Upselling and Cross-Selling as Instruments

The beauty of subscription relationships lies in their potential for growth. Your subscribers have taken the first step, immersed in the initial offering. Now, it's time to orchestrate the climb to a crescendo. Upselling and cross-selling become your instruments, playing harmoniously to expand the subscriber's experience. As they immerse themselves in your offerings, their appetite for more naturally awakens. Each interaction becomes a chance to introduce new offerings, enhancing their experience and your revenue.

Apple Music exemplifies this by offering a basic music streaming subscription. As subscribers become accustomed to the service, Apple introduces higher-tier plans that include more features like lossless audio or spatial audio support. This climb to crescendo through upselling adds layers of value, enticing subscribers to explore advanced offerings and enhancing their overall experience.

Rhapsody of Engagement: The Ongoing Serenade

Imagine each subscription as a key that unlocks an ongoing serenade. With every new interaction, you're composing a rhapsody of engagement. From exclusive content to personalized recommendations, you're building a narrative that keeps subscribers immersed and captivated. Each touchpoint becomes a stanza, adding depth and resonance to the subscriber's journey. It's not just about retaining them; it's about enveloping them in an enchanting narrative that evolves and deepens over time.

Each subscription payment isn't just transactional; it's an invitation to an ongoing serenade. Take Birchbox, for instance, which sends subscribers a monthly box of beauty samples. This rhapsody of engagement isn't limited to products; it's an experience. Birchbox engages subscribers with tailored product recommendations, beauty tutorials, and exclusive member events, creating a narrative that goes beyond the products themselves.

Taming the Tempest: Subscription Model Challenges

Cost of Entry: The Symphony of Investment

Embarking on the subscription journey resembles orchestrating a grand spectacle. The allure of recurring revenue harmonizes with the need for a substantial upfront investment. This symphony demands resources, from marketing to promotions, strategic partnerships to technological infrastructures. Consider the inception of the New York Times digital subscription. The venerable newspaper recognized the digital shift and invested in creating a seamless online reading experience, bolstered by multimedia content and investigative journalism. The cost of entry is the overture that sets the tone for the entire performance, demanding a harmonious balance of capital and creativity.

Farewell, Subscribers: Navigating the Churn Chorus

In the world of subscriptions, churn is an ever-lurking shadow, capable of disrupting even the most harmonious of business melodies. Just ask gym subscriptions or digital news outlets. Mitigating churn requires vigilant monitoring, personalized retention strategies, and adapting offerings to evolving subscriber needs. Netflix, recognizing the importance of original content, invests heavily to keep subscribers engaged and minimize the temptation to cancel. Netflix's commitment to a constant influx of new shows and movies serves as a defensive strategy, enhancing loyalty and diminishing the chances of subscribers bidding farewell.

Perceived Value Enigma: Sustaining the Elegance

In this dance, maintaining the allure of value is a quest that cannot be taken lightly. Subscribers must perceive continued benefit beyond the initial excitement. Amazon Prime constantly strives to uphold this allure, ensuring that the value derived from shipping perks, streaming services, and exclusive deals far outweighs the subscription cost. The annual Prime Day event, for instance, serves as an ingenious way to add perceived value, offering exclusive discounts to subscribers. Balancing perceived value with pricing is a delicate dance that can make or break a subscription offering, influencing how subscribers view their ongoing commitment.

Saturation Siren: Standing Out in a Sea of Subscriptions

Amid a sea of subscriptions, standing out isn't a gentle lullaby—it's a battle cry. With each passing day, more businesses join the subscription symphony, creating a saturation siren that demands innovation. For instance, the meal kit delivery industry experienced explosive growth, but not all survived. Blue Apron, an early entrant, faced saturation challenges as competitors flooded the market. To thrive, businesses must differentiate through unique offerings, impeccable service, or exceptional experiences. Blue Apron, in response, diversified its menu, offered customization options, and focused on educating subscribers about cooking techniques. The result was a unique value proposition that distinguished them in a crowded space.

Quality Overture: Crafting a Seamless Experience

From the first chord to the finale, the quality of the subscription experience must crescendo without a sour note. Apple's success story lies in their commitment to quality. The Apple Music subscription isn't just about streaming; it's about delivering flawless sound quality, intuitive user interfaces, and curated playlists that resonate with subscribers. Quality is the overture that captures hearts and maintains the symphony of loyalty. Apple's meticulous attention to detail extends to every facet of the subscription experience, from the interface design to the clarity of sound, creating a harmonious experience that's unrivaled in the industry.

In the tumultuous sea of subscription challenges, these stories exemplify the harmonies of resilience and innovation. Just as a maestro guides the orchestra through crescendos and diminuendos, businesses must navigate these challenges with strategic finesse. By mastering the nuances of cost, churn, value, saturation, and quality, subscription models can resonate with customers and create melodies of success that leave audiences wanting more.

Choreography of Success: Designing Your Subscription Echelon

Ballet of Segmentation: Know your audience like a dance partner, moving in sync with their desires.

Just as a dancer knows every move of their partner, businesses must intimately understand their audience. Consider Spotify's brilliant segmentation strategy. By offering different subscription tiers catering to various needs, from casual listeners to audiophiles, they ensure each subscriber finds their rhythm. This ballet of segmentation allows subscribers to select the tier that aligns with their preferences, creating a personalized dance that keeps them engaged and loyal.

Price Waltz: Pricing isn't just a number; it's the rhythm that resonates with the soul of your subscriber.

Pricing isn't a monotonous figure; it's the tempo that shapes the dance. Take HBO Max's pricing strategy. They offer tiers with varying price points, each reflecting the breadth of content offered. The price waltz isn't just about cost; it's about finding the rhythm that harmonizes with perceived value. The balance between price and value is a delicate choreography that impacts subscribers' perception of what they're receiving.

Interlude of Trial: Offer a glimpse, a taste, a fleeting touch; let them feel the enchantment before they fully commit.

The interlude of trial is a dance of seduction. Amazon Prime's 30-day free trial, for instance, allows potential subscribers to dip their toes into the pool of benefits. This glimpse into the world of convenience, savings, and streaming content often leads to full commitment. The trial interlude is the moment where curiosity transforms into captivation, turning hesitant observers into enthusiastic participants.

Support Pas de Deux: When subscribers stumble, ensure your support catches them in a graceful embrace.

In this dance, stumbles are inevitable. The support pas de deux is where businesses showcase their grace. Apple's customer service for AppleCare+ subscribers is a prime example. When a device encounters trouble, Apple's support offers a graceful embrace, resolving issues swiftly and ensuring a seamless experience. This support dance isn't just about troubleshooting; it's about rekindling confidence and loyalty.

Innovation Symphony: Let each act be a crescendo, an ode to perpetual evolution, surprising and delighting subscribers.

The subscription dance must evolve to stay captivating. Disney+ exemplifies this with the introduction of "Premier Access," where subscribers can access new movie releases for an additional fee. This innovation symphony creates a buzz, enticing subscribers with fresh, exclusive experiences. The dance of innovation ensures that each act is a crescendo, a step forward that keeps subscribers engaged and excited.

Churn Ballet: Oh, the intricate dance to prevent the curtain from falling. Special offers, exclusive content – keep the audience enthralled.

The churn ballet is the dance to retain subscribers, preventing the final curtain from falling. Consider Dropbox's approach. When users are at risk of churning, Dropbox offers them an additional free space, a special incentive to stay. This dance is all about offering special offers, exclusive content, or personalized experiences that remind subscribers of the value they'll miss if they leave. It's a dynamic choreography that keeps subscribers enthralled and engaged, prolonging their subscription journey.

The choreography of subscription success involves intricate moves, each tailored to keep subscribers enchanted. Just as a dance performance captivates an audience, a well-designed subscription model entices, engages, and resonates. Through segmentation, pricing, trials, support, innovation, and churn management, businesses choreograph a symphony that resonates deeply with subscribers, ensuring they remain front-row spectators in the ongoing dance of value and engagement.

Chronicles of Subscription: Tales of Transformation

In a world where traditional business models held sway, a new narrative emerged - one of triumph born from the subscription revolution. This anthology unveils the stories of enterprises that embraced the unconventional, challenging the norms, and rewriting the annals of commerce. Through counterintuitive choices and strategic audacity, these entities wove sagas of subscription-driven evolution that resonate through the ages.

The Journey Begins: Netflix's Odyssey of Streaming Dominion

In the hushed corridors of history, a paradigm shift unfurled, scripted by none other than Netflix. From its humble origins as a DVD-by-Mail marvel, Netflix defied expectations. As the world clung to tangible DVDs, Netflix cast its eyes to the digital horizon. With the swiftness of a shooting star, they ushered in the era of streaming. Their gamble paid off in subscribers aplenty - a global tapestry woven with over 200 million threads, each a testament to their audacious foray into the unknown. By sowing the seeds of innovation, Netflix redefined media, showing that even the most successful molds could be shattered for a triumphant rebirth.

Harmonizing the Unfamiliar: Amazon Prime's Symphony of Value

In the age-old marketplace, Amazon Prime orchestrated a symphony of loyalty through bundled delights. Against all odds, Amazon defied conventional wisdom. In a world of individualism, they intertwined shipping, streaming, and exclusive treasures into a single ensemble.

The sum of the parts was greater than the whole, and the Amazon Prime anthem reverberated through the hearts of 200 million subscribers. In this breathtaking crescendo, Amazon taught the world that a holistic composition could strike chords of unwavering allegiance, rewriting the sheet music of subscription success.

Brushstrokes of Transformation: Adobe's Canvas of Software Evolution

In the realm of creativity, Adobe wielded a brush of subscription innovation. Their canvas was the world of software, once tethered to ownership. But Adobe dared to reimagine this canvas, splashing it with continuous access instead. Their counterintuitive stroke turned ripples into waves, amassing 22 million subscribers in a masterpiece of subscription metamorphosis. In the end, Adobe's tale whispered that evolution and disruption could harmonize in vibrant unison, birthing subscription marvels from the ashes of the past.

Epic Odyssey of Fitness: Peloton's Quest for Connection

In the empire of fitness, Peloton embarked on an epic subscription odyssey. While the world trod the path of gymnasiums, Peloton charted its own course. It wove the tapestry of immersive fitness experiences, delivering workouts through screens, transcending the limits of space and time. With each pedal and stretch, Peloton fused technology and sweat into a communion of subscribers. They transformed solitary fitness into a dance of connected souls, affirming that even the most disparate realms could become one in the embrace of subscription communion.

Legends on Two Wheels: Harley-Davidson's Symphony of Subscriptions

In the annals of motorcycling, Harley-Davidson roared with a symphony of innovation. Tradition met transformation as Harley-Davidson ushered motorcycles into the age of subscriptions.

Revving in defiance of the past, subscribers cruised through a world without ownership, embodying the spirit of exploration. Through this radical shift, the roar of motorcycles was not merely heard but felt by a diverse audience. Harley-Davidson's tale painted a vivid picture of how legacy industries could rewrite their narrative with subscription ink.

Spells of Enchantment: Disney+ and the Streaming Spell

In the land of entertainment, Disney+ cast a spell of content-driven subscription magic. Amidst the streaming tumult, Disney boldly took the stage. Armed with beloved franchises, they conjured a kingdom of nostalgia, bewitching over 100 million subscribers in mere moments. Their sorcery unveiled that even in a realm teeming with giants, unique content could carve a niche as deep as the imagination itself.

Ink of the Mind: The New York Times' Digital Journalistic Odyssey

In the realm of ink and truth, The New York Times embarked on a digital odyssey of subscriptions. In a world awash with free words, they chose the uncharted path - charging for digital news. The very notion was anathema, yet The New York Times understood that the sustenance of journalism required an investment. They poured the essence of in-depth analysis and exclusive narratives into their inkwell, attracting a loyal readership that revered quality. Through this paradox, they etched an indelible lesson that counterintuitive choices could pen tales of longevity.

Threads of Elegance: Rent the Runway's Subscription Couture

In the world of fashion, Rent the Runway wove threads of subscription elegance. Amidst the tide of ownership, they unveiled a new fabric - one of renting clothing. Defying norms, they offered fleeting moments of couture without the burden of permanence. In this tapestry, occasional fashion became an anthem, resonating with souls who sought variety over constancy.

Professional Sonnets: LinkedIn Premium's Symphony of Networking

In the arena of professionalism, LinkedIn Premium composed a sonnet of subscription enhancement. In the age of free connections, they chose a different refrain. They offered a harmonious blend of tools for career elevation, crafting a symphony that resonated with professionals willing to invest in their journey. Through this counterintuitive composition, LinkedIn Premium whispered that the crescendo of success could be orchestrated through subscription insight.

Gaming Chronicles: Microsoft's Virtual Odyssey

In the realm of gaming, Microsoft embarked on a virtual odyssey through Xbox Game Pass. Against the backdrop of individual game purchases, they unfurled a vast library of experiences for a single monthly key. The notion was paradoxical, yet the allure of variety transcended conventional wisdom. Through their digital realm, Microsoft redefined gaming by proving that subscription access could be more tantalizing than traditional ownership.

Culinary Verses: Graze's Subscription Feast

In the realm of gastronomy, Graze composed culinary verses with subscription delight. Against the aisle-studded norm, they curated a feast of healthier snacks, dished up through subscription boxes. This tapestry of counterintuitive convenience defied retail expectations, offering personalized nourishment at doorsteps. Graze's tale whispered that even the simplest pleasures could be revolutionized through unconventional thinking.

Epilogue: Echoes of Subscription Triumphs

And so, these tales, woven across industries, epochs, and ideals, converge in an epilogue of collective wisdom. From redefining the definition of media to challenging norms in fitness, journalism, fashion, and even snacking, these enterprises etched their names on the scroll of subscription triumphs. Amidst the symphony of counterintuitive choices, they proved that innovation, when intertwined with adaptability and customer insight, could forge melodies of loyalty, value, and engagement. These stories, penned with ink of audacity, will echo through the corridors of time, inspiring generations to challenge the ordinary and compose their own tales of subscription triumphs.

Subscription Stories: Lessons from Faltered Transitions

MoviePass: Fumbling in the Subscription Theater

Case Study: In the grand theater of moviegoing, MoviePass took the stage with the audacious goal of transforming the audience's experience through an unlimited movie ticket subscription.

Failure: Launched in 2011, MoviePass captured the spotlight, attracting millions of subscribers with the promise of endless cinema outings for a flat monthly fee. However, the applause turned to gasps as the curtains revealed the underlying flaws. The unsustainable pricing model cast a shadow over the company's financial health. The constant shifts in pricing, restrictions, and terms left the audience bewildered, damaging customer trust. As a crescendo of chaos built, subscribers fled the theater, leading MoviePass to a final act of bankruptcy in 2019.

Analysis: The somber notes of MoviePass's failure were echoes of unsustainable pricing. By offering an all-you-can-watch buffet of movies, the company faced financial ruin as avid cinephiles capitalized on the opportunity to attend screenings daily. High operational costs, driven by the frequency of usage, created a discordant financial symphony. Moreover, the company's inconsistent communication and alterations to subscription terms shattered the harmony with subscribers, eroding the loyalty that underpins successful subscriptions. A wiser approach would have been to introduce tiered pricing structures based on usage, setting clear expectations from the start, and nurturing a sustainable financial model that could have danced to the tune of long-term viability.

Quibi: The Brief Symphony of Subscription Quandary

Case Study: Quibi took the stage in 2020 with a mobile platform designed to revolutionize short-form content through subscription-based, high-quality, bite-sized videos.

Failure: The opening act held promise, with significant investments and star-studded content. However, the spotlight quickly dimmed as Quibi's performance floundered. Despite a fervent entrance, the audience engagement never crescendoed. The audience's attention remained fixed on established platforms while Quibi's content struggled to find its rhythm. The finale was swift – within a year, the curtain fell as Quibi faced insurmountable challenges, bowing out from the subscription stage.

Analysis: Quibi's composition fell flat due to an incomplete understanding of the audience's desires. The company's assumption that users would gladly pay for short-form content was a dissonant note in an era of abundant free alternatives. Furthermore, Quibi's content lacked the distinct melody needed to stand out in a cacophony of online video offerings. The lack of a clear differentiation from established platforms like YouTube and TikTok deprived Quibi of a unique selling point. The orchestra of success requires comprehensive market research, a compelling content strategy that resonates with the intended audience, and a resonant value proposition that creates a distinctive chord in the subscription symphony.

These cautionary tales illuminate the path to subscription success. The lessons are clear: a successful transition to a subscription model necessitates a finely-tuned composition. The overture should be one of meticulous planning, resonating with the audience's needs. The melody must be one of clear communication, cultivating trust and loyalty. The harmony should be one of sustainable pricing, avoiding discordant financial strains. Just as counterintuitive choices led to subscription triumphs in the past, careful navigation of these pitfalls can ensure that the subscription overture resonates harmoniously, creating a lasting melody of value, engagement, and subscriber satisfaction.

Navigating Unsuitable Waters: Business Models Less Suited for Subscriptions

While subscription models have been successful across various industries, there are certain business models that may not be well-suited for subscriptions due to their nature, consumer behavior, or market dynamics. Here are a few examples:

1. **One-time Purchase Products**: Businesses that primarily sell products that are used infrequently or have a long lifespan may not be ideal for subscriptions. For instance, purchasing a washing machine or a refrigerator doesn't align with the subscription model's recurring payment structure.

2. **Highly Seasonal Products**: Businesses dealing with products that are highly seasonal or have irregular usage patterns might not find subscriptions suitable. Subscribers may cancel during the off-season, leading to revenue instability.

3. **Low-frequency Services**: Services that are used sporadically or on an irregular basis, such as legal or medical consultations, may not align well with the recurring payment nature of subscriptions.

4. **Custom-made or Personalized Items**: Businesses that specialize in custom-made or personalized products may struggle with subscription models, as the uniqueness of each item may not fit the standardized subscription model.

5. **Commodity Products**: Businesses selling everyday commodity products like basic groceries or essentials might not find subscriptions beneficial due to the low differentiation and competitive pricing pressure.

6. **Highly Fragmented Markets**: In markets with numerous providers offering similar products or services, subscriptions may not stand out as a differentiating factor, leading to difficulties in customer acquisition and retention.

7. **Transactional Services**: One-time, transactional services like car repairs or plumbing might not naturally lend themselves to subscriptions, as they are often sought only when needed.

8. **Short-lived Trends**: Industries with rapidly changing trends might not be suited for subscriptions, as consumer preferences can evolve quickly, rendering the subscription offerings obsolete.

9. **Luxury Goods**: Businesses dealing with high-end luxury goods may find it challenging to offer subscription models that align with the exclusivity and prestige associated with their brand.

10. **High-Value, Low-Volume Sales**: Businesses that thrive on high-value, low-volume sales, such as real estate or high-end electronics, may not benefit from the subscription model's focus on smaller, recurring payments.

It's important to note that even in these cases, creative adaptations or hybrid models could still make subscriptions viable. The key is to carefully consider customer behavior, value proposition, and market dynamics before determining if a subscription model is appropriate for a particular business.

Navigating Unsuitable Waters

Adapting Business Models for Subscription Success

In the grand symphony of business models, there are those that initially seem discordant with the melodies of subscriptions. Yet, with a touch of innovation and a willingness to dance to a different rhythm, these models can find their harmonious notes. Let's explore how businesses can transform their tunes and thrive in the subscription arena:

1. **Hybrid Harmonies**: Blend the familiarity of traditional models with the allure of subscriptions. Imagine a luxury brand that offers an exclusive subscription tier, granting early access to new collections while preserving the mystique of limited-edition allure.

2. **Value Crescendo**: Elevate the symphony of products by appending value-added services. Picture a product with an irregular lifecycle – a subscription for maintenance and updates could infuse perpetual value, transforming a solitary purchase into an ongoing relationship.

3. **Seasonal Overture**: Embrace the ebb and flow of seasonality with limited-time subscriptions. Envision a business offering short bursts of subscription during peak periods, allowing customers to savor the essence of your offering when demand crescendos.

4. **Flexible Refrains**: For products that blend into the tapestry of daily life, offer flexible subscription options. Imagine a subscription that ebbs and flows with customer needs,

aligning with their usage patterns and celebrating the joy of custom rhythms.

5. **Membership Sonatas**: Craft membership programs that serenade customers with exclusive perks and benefits. Think of a program that offers a backstage pass to special events, letting subscribers revel in an ensemble of privileges.

6. **Bundle Finale**: For high-value, low-volume businesses, create crescendos of value with bundled subscription offerings. Envision a symphony of complementary products and services, resonating with customers who seek a grander symphony of offerings.

7. **Personalized Melodies**: Explore the enchantment of personalization for bespoke businesses. Consider a subscription tier that delivers tailor-made variations, as if composing a unique piece of music for each subscriber.

8. **Educational Interludes**: Transform low-frequency services into harmonious subscriptions with a touch of education. Picture a service that provides subscribers with ongoing insights and learning, resonating long after the initial transaction.

9. **Trend Tempos**: In an era of fleeting trends, create an opus of trial subscriptions. Envision a portal that offers the latest trends on-demand, allowing subscribers to dance to the tempo of the moment without a long-term commitment.

10. **Segmentation Serenades**: In a market with diverse notes, offer tiered subscription options that harmonize with varying customer preferences. Imagine a symphony of tiers, each resonating uniquely with a different audience.

11. **Collaborative Crescendos**: Harmonize with fellow artists by orchestrating collaborative subscription partnerships. Picture a business creating harmonious duets with complementary offerings, crafting a melodious ensemble of value.

12. **Adaptive Aria**: Listen to the feedback of your audience and evolve your subscription composition accordingly. Let the desires of your subscribers shape the melody, ensuring that the rhythm of your offering remains in tune with their desires.

With these adaptations, even the most unlikely candidates for subscription success can find their voice in the symphony of recurring revenue. Just as a skilled conductor guides an orchestra to new heights, businesses that embrace the art of adaptation can transform their models, making them sing in harmony with the melodies of subscriptions.

Summarizing the Symphony of Subscription Triumphs

Imagine a grand concert hall, where the stage is set for a symphony of subscription triumphs. Each section of the orchestra represents a different business or industry, and the conductor's baton symbolizes the visionary leaders who dared to challenge norms. As the conductor raises the baton, the symphony begins:

1. **Opening Movement: The Prelude of Possibilities**

   Netflix takes the lead with its transformation from a DVD rental service to a streaming powerhouse. The shift symbolizes the potential for disruptive innovation to redefine entire industries.

2. **Harmony of Value: Bundles and Beyond**

   Amazon Prime joins the orchestra, showing how bundled services can create a powerful harmony of value. The orchestra resonates with the idea that offering more than the sum of parts can foster deep loyalty.

3. **Rhythms of Adaptation: Evolution through Subscriptions**

   Adobe's transformation from software ownership to subscription-based access adds a new rhythm. The orchestra highlights the importance of adapting to changing customer needs while challenging traditional paradigms.

4. **Chords of Connection: Immersive Experiences**

   Peloton introduces immersive fitness experiences, connecting individuals in a shared journey towards better health. The orchestra emphasizes the impact of creating communities and shared experiences through subscriptions.

5. **Bold Crescendo: Legacy Industries Reimagined**

Harley-Davidson's motorcycle subscription service and Rent the Runway's fashion subscription resonate as a bold crescendo. The orchestra showcases how legacy industries can innovate and find new avenues through subscriptions.

6. **Content Ensemble: Nurturing Niche Markets**

Disney+ captures hearts with content-driven subscriptions, demonstrating how unique offerings can create a captivating melody even in a competitive landscape. The orchestra reminds us of the power of specialized content to carve out a dedicated audience.

7. **Harmonious Insight: Counterintuitive Choices**

The New York Times' monetization of digital news and LinkedIn Premium's elevated networking demonstrate the beauty of counterintuitive choices. The orchestra highlights the importance of challenging norms and finding untapped value.

8. **Digital Symphony: Transformation and Access**

Xbox Game Pass's library of games and Graze's curated snack deliveries add digital notes to the symphony. The orchestra emphasizes the transformative potential of subscriptions in reshaping industries and delivering convenience.

9. **Epilogue: Ongoing Melodies of Evolution**

The symphony concludes with a harmonious epilogue, reminding us that the world of subscription triumphs is ever evolving. The orchestra reflects the ongoing nature of innovation, adaptation, and the continuous pursuit of resonance with customers.

In this mental model, each element of the orchestra symbolizes a different aspect of subscription-driven success. The conductor represents visionary leaders who orchestrated these transformations, while the symphony itself encapsulates the diversity of industries, themes, and lessons that emerge from these stories. Just as a symphony is a harmonious blend of melodies, these subscription triumphs create a harmonious blend of innovation, value, and engagement that resonates with businesses and consumers alike.

Mental Model: The Symphony of Subscription Success Framework

Imagine a mental framework that guides enterprises on their journey towards subscription triumphs. This framework is a symphony composed of distinct movements, each representing a crucial step to orchestrate a successful subscription-based business model. As you follow this model, you'll craft your unique symphony of value, engagement, and growth.

1. **Harmonizing Vision: Defining Your Narrative**

   Begin by envisioning your enterprise's future. Choose a clear theme, like evolution, personalization, or convenience, that will resonate with your audience. This movement sets the tone for your symphony and gives direction to your subscription journey.

2. **Counterintuitive Prelude: Challenging Conventions**

   Break away from the norm. Identify an aspect of your industry or service that can be reimagined. Like Netflix's shift from DVDs to streaming, consider a bold pivot that challenges established models. This unexpected twist will set you apart and intrigue your audience.

3. **Value Sonata: Crafting Bundled Delights**

   Compose a symphony of value by bundling services, features, or products. Like Amazon Prime, intertwine offerings to create a holistic experience that's more compelling than individual parts. Harmonize diverse elements to create a harmonious whole that resonates with subscribers.

4. **Engagement Movement: Creating Immersive Experiences**

   Design interactions that immerse subscribers in your world. Like Peloton, offer experiences that transcend the transactional, fostering connections and community. The rhythm of engagement should evoke emotions and build lasting relationships.

5. **Innovation Fugue: Rethinking Norms**

   Challenge norms within your industry. Consider legacy models, like Harley-Davidson's motorcycle subscription. Break down barriers and reimagine traditional concepts. This movement should highlight how your unique offering can change perceptions and behaviors.

6. **Content Overture: Nurturing Unique Narratives**

   Cultivate content that resonates deeply with your target audience, much like Disney+. Develop narratives that embody your brand's identity and values. These stories will become an integral part of your subscription symphony, creating a loyal following.

7. **Strategic Interlude: Embracing Counterintuitive Choices**

   Embrace counterintuitive decisions that align with your vision. Like The New York Times' monetization of digital news, challenge industry norms. These strategic choices should be guided by a keen understanding of customer needs and an unwavering commitment to excellence.

8. **Evolving Sonata: Transforming through Technology**

   Integrate technology to transform your offering, like Xbox Game Pass's digital library. Leverage digital solutions to enhance convenience, accessibility, and customization. This movement should showcase your enterprise's ability to evolve with the digital age.

9. **Finale of Sustainability: Responsible Growth**

   Conclude your symphony by acknowledging the responsibility of sustainability, as seen in Graze's curated snacks. Demonstrate your commitment to ethical practices, environmental consciousness, and responsible growth. This closing movement ensures a harmonious legacy.

10. **Epilogue: Ongoing Melodies of Innovation**

    Remember that the symphony never truly ends. Like the epilogue of our framework, your journey toward subscription triumphs is ongoing. Continuously refine, innovate, and adapt. Allow your symphony to evolve, resonating with new audiences and pioneering trends.

In this mental framework, each movement represents a critical step that contributes to the harmonious symphony of subscription success. By following this model, enterprises can weave their unique narrative, embracing innovation, value, and engagement in a way that resonates deeply with subscribers and guides them towards triumphant subscription offerings.

Final Encore

In a world of business sonatas and operatic strategies, the Subscription Model stands as a maestro. A duet of profit and loyalty, it's not just a part but a saga, an epic of continual engagement. Yet, it's a dance on a tightrope, where balance is the true virtuoso. With the rhythm of challenge and the melody of innovation, businesses can conduct the orchestra of Subscription Revenue and carve their name in the symphony of success.

Interludes of Inspiration: The Evolving Landscape of Subscription Triumphs

As the stories of subscription triumphs unfold, they cast light on a broader landscape of evolving paradigms. These interludes provide insights into the overarching themes and trends that have emerged from the subscription-driven revolution, shaping industries and consumer behavior alike.

The Symphony of Data: Unveiling Personalization

Amidst the crescendo of subscriptions, a silent symphony of data orchestration emerged. With each subscription, a torrent of preferences, behaviors, and insights flowed. Businesses, armed with this data, composed personalized experiences that resonated deeply with subscribers. From Netflix's algorithmic recommendations to LinkedIn's tailored insights, personalization became the crescendo of subscription offerings. In this era, the once-untouched corners of consumer desires were brought to the forefront, harmonizing individual experiences with the grand orchestra of subscriptions.

Metamorphosis of Ownership: From Possession to Access

The age-old concept of ownership underwent a metamorphosis in the wake of subscriptions. As exemplified by Harley-Davidson and Rent the Runway, the notion of possessing shifted towards the allure of access. The tangible gave way to the ephemeral, as subscribers sought experiences over ownership. This transformation questioned the very nature of ownership, ushering in a new dawn where the value lay not in possession, but in the freedom of choice and the allure of variety.

The Canvas of Convenience: A Tapestry of Seamless Experiences

Across subscription tales, a common thread emerged - the canvas of convenience painted with bold strokes. From Amazon Prime's bundled ease to Graze's doorstep delivery, these businesses catered to the modern consumer's hunger for frictionless experiences. The subscription model became a tapestry where convenience was not an afterthought, but a central motif that ensured subscribers' journey was as seamless as the rhythm of a symphony.

Boundaries of Imagination: Challenging Industry Norms

Within these narratives, an orchestra of boundary pushers stood out. Netflix and Disney+ redefined entertainment consumption, while Adobe and Microsoft reimagined software and gaming paradigms. These pioneers illustrated that industries once believed to be set in stone could be molded anew through counterintuitive choices. The lesson resounded - the limits of imagination could be stretched, and the notes of innovation could reshape even the most entrenched sectors.

The Value Mandala: Beyond Monetary Exchange

In the world of subscriptions, the exchange of monetary value was merely the prelude to a grander melody. As Amazon Prime and ClassPass showcased, the holistic value proposition extended beyond a mere financial transaction. Emotional bonds were woven, communities were nurtured, and well-being was prioritized. Subscribers were not just customers; they became part of an interconnected symphony, where the value extended far beyond the dollars exchanged.

Harmonizing the Future: Themes of Sustainability and Expansion

In the grand composition of subscription triumphs, themes of sustainability and global expansion rose like a crescendo. Businesses like Peloton and ClassPass transcended geographical borders, connecting communities worldwide through their subscription offerings. Meanwhile, concepts of sustainability echoed through Graze's curated snacks and the reduction of physical waste through digital content delivery. These themes underscored that subscription success resonates with the future's harmonious blend of global connectivity and responsible stewardship.

Coda: The Ongoing Symphony

As this part of subscription triumphs draws to a close, it is important to remember that the symphony continues to evolve. The orchestration of subscriptions is an ongoing endeavor, shaped by the dynamic interplay of technology, consumer preferences, and audacious visions. New melodies will be composed, and new ensembles will take the stage, each seeking to weave their own narrative of subscription triumph. In this symphony of innovation, the only constant is change, and the resonance of subscription models will continue to harmonize with the ever-evolving rhythms of commerce and human engagement.

Reflections

Strategies for Making the Most of the Subscription Economy

Strategy	Key Points
1. Help Customers Understand Your Value Proposition	Prospective customers should understand and experience what you offer. High barriers to entry can hinder sampling and reduce subscriber acquisition.
2. Optimize Customer Acquisition Costs	Efficiently acquiring subscribers is essential for subscription businesses." Balancing customer acquisition costs with lifetime value is crucial.
3. Foster Customer Engagement and Retention	Continuous engagement and retention efforts are vital in the subscription economy. Personalization, feedback loops, and added value enhance customer loyalty.

Subscription Business Models Are Great for Some Businesses and Terrible for Others

Key Points	Leaders	Laggards
Market/ Service Fit	Ensure market/service fit before investing in onboarding customers. Focus on designing the right offering.	Create a membership model solely for recurring revenue without considering value for members. Trust is critical.

Key Points	Leaders	Laggards
Metrics	Measure success with member churn and engagement rather than just customer acquisition and sales.	May prioritize short-term revenue gains over member treatment and long-term relationships.
Culture of Membership	Focus on building a culture of membership that values long-term relationships across the organization.	May not consider the implications of membership on sales, finance, and product development.
Member-Centric Approach	Love members more than products. Adapt offerings to meet members' evolving needs and goals.	May not adapt to changing member needs and preferences. May resist introducing new platforms.
Listening to Members	Listen to members, but don't let them drive strategic direction entirely. Balance their input with market research.	Avoid letting long-time members dictate strategy at the expense of incoming members and market trends.
Freemium Strategy	Use freemium as a trial, to create a networked effect, or as a marketing channel. Ensure it aligns with a larger business strategy.	Avoid offering memberships for free without a clear purpose (trial, network effect, marketing). Charging for something that used to be free can be challenging.
Focus on Long-Term Relationships	Change the business model to prioritize maintaining long-term relationships over quick customer acquisition.	May not adapt their business model to focus on long-term relationships, missing out on higher profitability and customer loyalty.

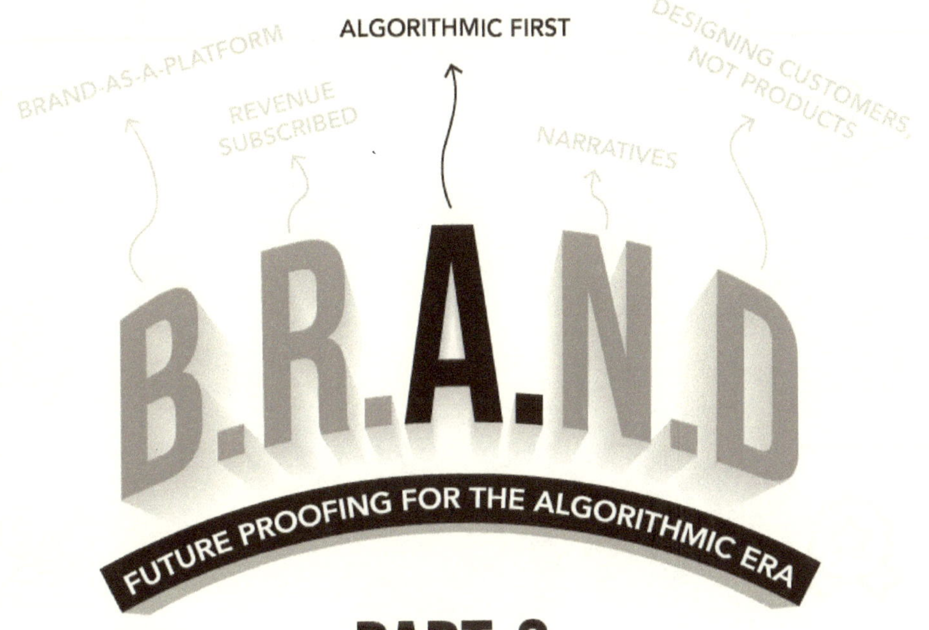

PART-3

ALGORITHMIC FIRST

CRAFTING EXPERIENCES BEYOND IMAGINATION

Crafting Experience Beyond Imagination

In the intricate weave of our digital age, algorithms stand as the masterful weavers crafting the fabric of our daily lives. They sift through oceans of data, making decisions that guide our choices, shape our experiences, and influence our perspectives. Yet, as algorithms increasingly dictate the contours of our reality, a crucial question emerges: What happens when the weavers' threads of code intertwine with the delicate fibers of human morality?

Here we venture into the heart of the ethical nexus that envelops algorithms. As we journey through the virtual landscapes of personalization, predictive insights, and immersive experiences, we find ourselves confronted with a profound challenge: How do we navigate the labyrinth of algorithmic morality? In this part, we unravel the complex tapestry of ethical considerations, revealing the profound implications that algorithms have on our values, society, and the very essence of what it means to be human.

With each click, swipe, and recommendation, algorithms make choices that ripple through the digital and physical realms. But what lies beneath these choices? What values, biases, and ethical frameworks inform the decisions made by lines of code? Join us as we embark on a contemplative exploration, where we shed light on the intricate dance between algorithms and morality. From the illumination of hidden biases to the dawn of algorithmic fairness, we traverse the blurred boundaries between data-driven precision and the nuanced world of ethics.

As we venture deeper, we'll encounter the thorny thickets of algorithmic transparency, the tightrope walks between personalization and privacy, and the sobering effects of algorithmic discrimination. We'll peer into the ethical mirrors of predictive analytics, where glimpses of potential futures raise questions of autonomy and consent. In the age of algorithmic power, we ponder who decides the symphony of values that shapes our shared reality.

So, fasten your seatbelts, for we're about to embark on a journey that challenges our perceptions, ignites our moral compass, and invites us to participate in the ongoing dialogue that navigates the crossroads of algorithmic morality. Welcome to a part that dares to untangle the intricate threads that bind algorithms and ethics, where we strive for a harmonious convergence that honors both technological advancement and the timeless values that define our humanity.

In the wild landscape of technology, the rules are constantly being rewritten, and algorithms? They are the rock stars rewriting them. Picture this part as a backstage pass to the heart of the digital action. From deciphering the cryptic language of algorithms to understanding how they shape what we see, buy, and explore, we're diving deep into the data-driven cosmos. Buckle up for a journey that will have you questioning reality, embracing personalization, and witnessing algorithms as the artists crafting our digital dreams.

Decoding the Enigma: Algorithms Unleashed

The Wizards Behind the Digital Curtain

Ever felt like your computer knows you better than your best friend? You might want to give credit to the genius of algorithms. But what are they really? Forget the tech jargon; we're here to unravel the enigma. Imagine algorithms as the secret recipe that serves up a personalized digital feast just for you. We're about to pull back the curtain, break down the complex terms, and give you the backstage tour of how algorithms turn data into the magic that is your digital experience.

From Data to Destiny: The Algorithmic Storytellers

Buckle up because algorithms are the storytellers of the digital age. They know what you want to read, what you'll binge-watch, and even what you're going to buy before you do. How? It's all in the data. We're here to show you the magic behind the curtain, using examples like Netflix's uncanny ability to suggest your next favorite show. By dissecting the building blocks of algorithms, we're turning you into a digital Sherlock, ready to decode the patterns that make your online life tick.

Example: 'The Netflix Whisperer'

Ever wondered how Netflix knows exactly what you're in the mood to watch? Their recommendation algorithm is like a psychic movie buff. It scours your viewing history, tosses it into a mathematical cauldron, and voilà—out comes a selection of shows that seem to know you better than you know yourself. It's like having a best friend who's also a mind-reader, and it's all thanks to the algorithmic magic happening behind the scenes.

Mining Gold from Data: The Data Detective

In the digital realm, data is more precious than gold. Every click, every swipe, and every scroll generates a data trail that tells a story about you. We're delving into this goldmine, exploring the different types of data, where they come from, and how organizations harness them to understand you better than you understand yourself. Get ready to dive into a sea of information and discover the secret sauce that makes your digital experience one-of-a-kind.

Example: Amazon's Crystal Ball

Have you ever been baffled by Amazon's eerily accurate product recommendations? It's not magic; it's data-driven strategy at its finest. Amazon's algorithm crunches numbers faster than a calculator on steroids, analyzing your browsing history, purchases, and even what you hover over but don't buy. Then, like a psychic salesperson, it suggests products you didn't even know you needed. It's like having a personal shopper who knows your style better than you do.

The Art of Personalization: Custom-Made for You

Tailoring Reality to Your Tastes

Imagine a world where every digital experience is tailor-made just for you. Welcome to the world of personalization, where algorithms are the fashion designers crafting experiences that fit you like a glove. But hold on—it's not all rainbows and butterflies. We're diving into the ethics of personalization and privacy, ensuring you're not sacrificing too much for that perfect fit. Get ready to discover the balance between personalized perfection and your right to a digital secret garden.

The Personalization Puzzle: A Jigsaw of You

Your digital life is like a puzzle, and algorithms hold the pieces. From your search history to your social media posts, these puzzle pieces come together to create a digital portrait that's uniquely you. We're unpacking how algorithms use these fragments to assemble the perfect digital landscape, shaping what you see, hear, and experience. It's a puzzle that might just change the way you view your digital self.

Example: Spotify's Musical Crystal Ball

Spotify isn't just a music app; it's a musical fortune-teller. Its algorithm knows your musical tastes better than your closest friends. By analyzing your listening history, it's like having a DJ who knows what you're in the mood for even before you do. Whether you're feeling nostalgic or need a pump-up playlist, Spotify's algorithm is the ultimate party guest who knows exactly what jams to bring.

Bridging the Gap: Personalization vs. Privacy

Hold up—just because an algorithm knows what socks you like doesn't mean it should know your deepest secrets. We're tackling the ethics of personalization head-on. From the Cambridge Analytica scandal to the data breaches that make headlines, we're exploring the fine line between delightfully tailored experiences and the creepy feeling of being watched. It's time to demand personalization without compromising your digital dignity.

Example: Google's Tightrope Walk

Google walks the tightrope between personalization and privacy with its ads. It serves up ads based on your browsing history, but it's also giving you a backstage pass to control what data you share. From the Ad Settings page to the Incognito mode, Google's balancing act ensures that while you get personalized ads, you're still the one holding the strings to your data puppet.

The Renaissance of Human-Centered Algorithms

Wait, aren't algorithms supposed to replace humans? Not quite. We're diving into the world of "Human-Centered AI," where algorithms aren't the stars of the show—they're the supporting actors making sure you shine. From aiding designers in creating stunning visuals to helping doctors diagnose illnesses, algorithms are the sidekicks that make our human capabilities reach new heights. Get ready to meet the new dynamic duo—humans and algorithms, hand in virtual hand.

Example: Picasso's Algorithmic Muse

Algorithms aren't just for sci-fi movies; they're collaborating with artists too. In fact, algorithms have taken the art world by storm. Artists are using algorithms to generate stunning visuals, pushing the boundaries of creativity. For example, the "DeepDream" algorithm turns ordinary photos into surreal, dream-like masterpieces. It's not about replacing artists; it's about expanding the canvas of human imagination with algorithmic brushes.

Example: Health Care's Digital Partner

Algorithms aren't just here to help you find the perfect playlist—they're revolutionizing healthcare too. Take IBM's Watson, for instance. This AI-powered system is like having a team of doctors at your disposal, analyzing medical data faster than humanly possible. From diagnosing rare diseases to suggesting treatment plans, algorithms are lending a digital hand to doctors, ensuring patients receive the best care possible.

Crafting Tomorrow's Reality: The Future of Algorithmic Experiences

Envisioning the Digital Frontier

Get ready to gaze into the crystal ball of technology because we're peeking into the future. In this section, we're exploring how algorithms will continue to shape our lives. From augmented reality to predictive algorithms, we're venturing into the uncharted territory of what's to come. Strap in for a journey that will leave you both excited and slightly unnerved about the algorithmic wonders that lie ahead.

Beyond the Screen: Algorithms in Augmented Reality

Hold up your smartphone, and suddenly, the world transforms into a playground of digital enchantment. Welcome to the world of augmented reality (AR), where algorithms take what you see and sprinkle it with a dash of digital magic. We're exploring how algorithms create these parallel universes and enhance our reality in ways that were once confined to science fiction.

Example: Pokémon Go's AR Adventure

Remember the Pokémon Go crazy? It wasn't just a game; it was an AR revolution. By blending the real world with digital creatures, the game showcased how algorithms could make fantasy a part of everyday life. Suddenly, parks and streets became hunting grounds for virtual creatures, and millions of players embarked on real-world quests powered by algorithmic magic.

Predictive Power: Algorithms as Fortune-Tellers

What if you could predict the future? While we can't see into crystal balls, algorithms can predict trends, behaviors, and even your next online purchase. We're delving into the world of predictive algorithms, where data-driven insights anticipate what you'll do before you even know it. From forecasting stock prices to suggesting what book you might want to read next; algorithms are the modern-day Nostradamus.

Example: The Amazon Crystal Ball

Ever notice how Amazon seems to know what you're thinking? That's predictive algorithms at work. By analyzing your past purchases, searches, and even the time of day, Amazon's algorithm can predict what you might want to buy before you've even considered it. It's like having a virtual shopping assistant who can read your mind, ensuring you never run out of things to add to your cart.

Ethics in the Algorithmic Era: Navigating the Unknown

With great algorithmic power comes great ethical responsibility. In this part's finale, we're tackling the ethical dilemmas that arise in an algorithm-driven world. From algorithmic biases to the potential for digital manipulation, we're exploring the darker side of algorithms. It's time to ensure that as algorithms shape our future, they do so in ways that respect our humanity and safeguard our rights.

Example: Bias in Algorithmic Justice

Algorithms aren't immune to human biases; in fact, they can amplify them. From facial recognition software that struggles to identify people of color to algorithms that determine prison sentences, bias can seep into the digital realm. It's a wake-up call that reminds us that while algorithms are powerful, they're only as fair as the data that feeds them. Recognizing and rectifying these biases is essential to building a just algorithmic future.

Conclusion: Charting a Responsible Path into the Algorithmic Future

As we stand on the brink of a digital revolution, the power and potential of algorithms to transform our world is undeniable. Our journey through 'Crafting Tomorrow's Reality: The Future of Algorithmic Experiences' has opened our eyes to the myriad ways in which algorithms will shape our future. From the whimsical realms of augmented reality, as exemplified by the Pokémon Go phenomenon, to the predictive prowess of algorithms that foretell our needs and preferences, the influence of these digital architects is far-reaching.

However, with this immense power comes an equally significant responsibility. The ethical implications of algorithmic decision-making cannot be overstated. As we have seen, algorithms, while revolutionary, are not infallible. They can perpetuate biases and create new forms of digital divide if not carefully managed. The challenge ahead is to harness the potential of algorithms while vigilantly guarding against their misuse.

In conclusion, the future of algorithmic experiences is a tapestry of immense possibilities, interwoven with cautionary threads. It is a future that demands our keen attention, ethical consideration, and active participation. As we move forward, it is crucial to ensure that these digital innovations serve to enhance, not diminish, the human experience, and that they are guided by principles that uphold equity, fairness, and respect for all. Our journey into the algorithmic future is not just about embracing technological advancements; it's about shaping a world where technology works for the betterment of society.

Taming the Algorithmic Wilds: Forging Your Own Path

Introduction: Navigating the Maze of Algorithms

Alright, time to gear up for some algorithmic exploration! We're entering the unpredictable jungle of algorithms, where twists and turns await at every corner. In this section, we're arming you with the ultimate survival guide to hacking through this digital wilderness. From mastering the algorithmic terrain to guarding your virtual campfire, get ready to become the ultimate algorithmic trailblazer.

The Algorithmic Survival Gear: Equipping Yourself

Just like a warrior doesn't step into battle without gear, you can't venture into the algorithmic wilds without your toolkit. We're handing you a power-packed arsenal of knowledge and skills to tackle algorithms head-on. Unravel their codes, demystify the jargon, and learn the ropes of digital security. With these tools in your backpack, you'll be ready to conquer the algorithmic landscape like a true digital warrior.

Example: The Data Maze

Ever felt lost in the labyrinth of data privacy? You're not alone. We're lighting a torch to guide you through this maze. From understanding cookies to deciphering user agreements, we're empowering you to take charge of your data destiny. Navigate through the data jungle and emerge as a data-savvy adventurer who doesn't get tangled in the weeds of digital surveillance.

Surviving the Ethical Wilderness: Carving Your Path

In this uncharted algorithmic wilderness, ethics are your compass. We're venturing into the heart of ethical challenges that arise when algorithms call the shots. From bias in AI to the consequences of your online choices, we're arming you with the moral machete you need to hack through the ethical thicket. It's time to sculpt your own moral map and blaze a trail that's true to your values.

Example: The Virtue Dilemma

Imagine an algorithm that can distinguish between good and evil. It sounds like a superhero's power, right? But it's not that simple. We're delving into the complexities of developing moral algorithms. As AI evolves, the debate about whether machines can possess virtue intensifies. By grappling with these intricacies, you'll be prepared to navigate the ethical jungle without getting lost in the thick undergrowth of moral ambiguity.

Shielding Your Digital Campfire: Security Strategies

In the wild, a roaring campfire keeps predators at bay. In the digital realm, strong security keeps cyber threats in check. We're handing you a virtual shield to protect your online sanctuary. From creating unbreakable passwords to spotting digital traps, we're training you to be a cybersecurity ranger. With your guard up and defenses strong, you'll ensure that your digital campfire burns bright and secure.

Example: Phishermen of the Web

Ever encountered phishing hooks while swimming in the vast sea of the internet? It's time to sharpen your phishing-spotting skills. We're unveiling the tactics of cyber tricksters who lure unsuspecting prey into their nets. By recognizing their bait and steering clear of their hooks, you'll emerge as a cyber-savvy angler who doesn't fall for the deceitful dance of the phishermen.

Conclusion: Embrace Your Inner Algorithmic Explorer

As we emerge from the heart of the algorithmic wilderness, it's time to celebrate the fearless explorer within you. From deciphering algorithms' secrets to grappling with their ethical challenges and safeguarding your digital haven, you've transformed into a true algorithmic trailblazer. Remember, the digital realm is your playground, and algorithms are your tools. With your newfound knowledge, ethical compass, and security prowess, you're equipped to conquer the ever-evolving landscapes of algorithms and craft a digital adventure beyond imagination.

Collaborating with the Algorithmic Symphony: Shaping a Harmonious Future

Introduction: Orchestrating the Algorithmic Symphony

Prepare to step onto the conductor's podium, because in this section, we're diving into the realm of collaboration between humans and algorithms. Just as a symphony combines different instruments to create beautiful music, we're exploring how humans and algorithms can join forces to compose a harmonious future. Get ready to explore the potential of teamwork between our creative minds and the algorithmic maestros.

The Art of Co-Creation: Humans and Algorithms Unite

Imagine a world where human ingenuity and algorithmic prowess intertwine to craft masterpieces beyond imagination. In this part, we're exploring the magic of co-creation. From collaborating with AI to design stunning visuals to using algorithms to enhance our cognitive abilities, we're unraveling the possibilities of teamwork between the human spirit and the algorithmic muse.

Example: The Collaborative Canvas

Artists are no longer solitary creators; they're collaborating with algorithms to paint breathtaking canvases. We're diving into the world of generative art, where algorithms become the paintbrushes of human imagination. Through examples like "AIVA," an AI that composes symphonies, we're witnessing how the human-algorithm partnership births new forms of creativity that neither could achieve alone.

Augmented Intelligence: Elevating Human Capabilities

Ever wondered what happens when humans and algorithms combine their strengths? We're lifting the curtain on the concept of augmented intelligence. Instead of pitting humans against machines, we're exploring how algorithms can enhance our cognitive powers. From aiding doctors in diagnosing diseases to helping researchers crunch through complex data, we're witnessing a collaborative dance that propels human capabilities to new heights.

Example: Doctor Algorithm

Meet the medical marvels—algorithms that empower doctors with superhuman diagnostic abilities. Through case studies like "IDx-DR," an algorithm capable of detecting diabetic retinopathy, we're witnessing how algorithms are becoming medical sidekicks. By analyzing medical images and data, they're enabling doctors to make faster, more accurate diagnoses and revolutionizing patient care.

Ethics in Algorithmic Collaboration:

Conducting a Moral Symphony When humans and algorithms collaborate, ethics play a vital role in ensuring the harmony remains intact. In this section, we're delving into the ethical considerations that arise when our creative sparks merge with algorithmic fire. From ensuring transparency in AI-generated content to addressing questions of authorship, we're orchestrating a moral symphony that resonates with both human values and algorithmic capabilities.

Example: The Ghost in the Algorithm

Imagine reading a compelling news article, only to find out it was generated by an algorithm. We're exploring the realm of AI-generated content, where questions of authorship, credibility, and transparency come to the forefront. By acknowledging the presence of the algorithmic "ghostwriters," we're shaping an ethical landscape that respects the collaborative efforts behind the content we consume.

Conclusion: A Duet for the Ages

As we conclude this symphony of collaboration, it's time to savor the harmonious melody of humans and algorithms working together. From co-creating stunning art to amplifying human intelligence, we've witnessed the birth of a new creative paradigm. Remember, the future isn't about humans versus machines—it's about harnessing the power of both to compose a masterpiece of progress and innovation. Armed with the knowledge of ethical considerations, you're poised to conduct this duet for the ages, crafting a future that's both inspiring and harmonious.

Beyond Horizons: Exploring the Frontiers of Algorithmic Innovation

Introduction: Embarking on an Algorithmic Odyssey

Prepare to set sail for uncharted waters, because in this segment, we're journeying into the unknown territories of algorithmic innovation. Just as explorers once navigated unexplored lands, we're delving into the realms of quantum computing, swarm intelligence, and more. Get ready to embark on an algorithmic odyssey that challenges the boundaries of what we thought was possible.

Quantum Leaps: Algorithms in the Quantum Realm

Hold onto your hats because we're entering the quantum playground. In this part, we're unraveling the potential of quantum computing. From unlocking exponential computing power to revolutionizing cryptography, we're diving into the quantum sea, where traditional bits transform into qubits, and algorithms evolve to solve problems previously deemed unsolvable.

Imagine a computer that solves complex problems in minutes, which would take classical computers millennia. Quantum supremacy is the tipping point where quantum computers outperform their classical counterparts. We're exploring Google's quantum supremacy experiment and the implications of this breakthrough for fields ranging from cryptography to drug discovery, showcasing how algorithms are evolving in the quantum realm.

Swarm Intelligence: Algorithms of Collective Brilliance

Ever marveled at the coordinated dance of a flock of birds? We're harnessing the wisdom of the swarm in this section. From exploring how ants find the shortest path to highlighting the power of crowdsourcing, we're unveiling the beauty of algorithms that emulate nature's harmony. Prepare to witness algorithms that mimic the collective brilliance of swarms, creating innovative solutions that emerge from collaborative intelligence.

Imagine solving complex problems by tapping into the collective knowledge of a diverse group of individuals. We're diving into the phenomenon of crowdsourcing, where algorithms channel the wisdom of crowds to generate creative solutions. Through examples like the "Foldit" game, where gamers solved a scientific protein-folding problem, we're discovering how algorithmic orchestration can turn individuals into a powerful collective force.

Algorithmic Ethics in the Unknown: Navigating Uncharted Waters

As we venture into these uncharted algorithmic waters, ethics remain our guiding star. In this part, we're tackling the moral dilemmas that arise with quantum computing's immense power and swarm intelligence's collaborative potential. From addressing ethical concerns about quantum cryptography to ensuring fairness in crowdsourced decision-making, we're charting an ethical course through the algorithmic unknown.

Quantum computing's power could break traditional cryptography, raising concerns about data security and privacy. We're exploring the ethical implications of quantum algorithms that can crack encryption, highlighting the need to balance innovation with security. As the quantum realm challenges our ethical compass, we're shaping an approach that safeguards both technological advancement and individual rights.

Conclusion: A New Dawn of Algorithmic Discovery

As we conclude this expedition into the frontiers of algorithmic innovation, it's time to reflect on the remarkable journey we've undertaken. From quantum leaps to collective brilliance, we've ventured into realms that once existed only in the realm of science fiction. Remember, the algorithmic frontier knows no bounds, and with each step forward, we shape a new dawn of discovery. Armed with ethical consciousness and a spirit of curiosity, you're now equipped to continue exploring, innovating, and redefining the boundaries of algorithmic possibility.

A Tapestry of Algorithmic Reflections: Perspectives and Provocations

Looking Back, Looking Forward:

In this reflective section, we're taking a moment to pause and contemplate the journey we've embarked upon. Just as an artist step back from their canvas to see their creation, we're stepping back from the narrative to explore diverse perspectives on the world of algorithms. From thought-provoking debates to contemplative insights, get ready to delve into a tapestry of reflections that deepen our understanding of this algorithmic odyssey.

Exploring the Influence of Algorithms on Perception:

A deep dive into the digital world presents a thorough exploration of the significant influence algorithms have on our perception of reality. It investigates how these algorithms mold our thoughts, behaviors, and the way we understand the world around us. The piece delves into the formation of filter bubbles on social media platforms and ventures into the uncanny domain of AI-generated art. Throughout, it highlights the dual role of algorithms as tools that both enlighten and distort our view of our increasingly digital existence.

Example: Reality Remix

Imagine algorithms subtly shaping the news you read and the posts you see, creating a personalized reality. We're examining the phenomenon of algorithmic bias, where algorithms inadvertently reinforce our existing beliefs and limit exposure to diverse perspectives. By acknowledging this altered lens, we're raising awareness about the need for algorithmic transparency and diversity of information.

The Human Equation: Humans as Architects of Algorithms

Are algorithms the ultimate creators, or are humans the true architects? In this section, we're pondering the role of human influence in algorithmic design. From teaching algorithms to discern right from wrong to imbuing them with cultural and moral values, we're exploring how humans shape algorithms and, in turn, how algorithms shape us.

Imagine coding ethical principles into algorithms, guiding their decision-making. We're diving into the concept of moral AI, where algorithms are designed to make morally sound choices. Through examples like self-driving cars that must navigate ethical dilemmas, we're reflecting on the responsibility of embedding human values into algorithms and contemplating the implications of AI-powered moral decisions.

Navigating Uncertainty: Embracing the Algorithmic Unknown

As algorithms continue to evolve, uncertainty becomes our constant companion. In this section, we're embracing the unknown by acknowledging that the algorithmic journey is a perpetual exploration. From the potential pitfalls of overreliance on algorithms to the limitless possibilities of AI's evolution, we're navigating the algorithmic landscape with humility and a willingness to learn.

Imagine an AI that suddenly exhibits behavior it wasn't explicitly programmed for. We're delving into the world of unintended consequences, where algorithms surprise their creators. Through cases like Microsoft's "Tay" chatbot, we're recognizing that algorithms can behave unpredictably, reflecting the complexity of the human-machine relationship and urging us to approach algorithmic innovation with caution.

Conclusion: Threads of Reflection in the Algorithmic Tapestry

As we weave together the threads of these reflective perspectives, we're creating a rich and nuanced tapestry that enriches our understanding of the algorithmic journey. From altered perceptions to human influence and the embrace of uncertainty, we've explored the diverse facets of algorithms that shape our digital lives. Remember, the algorithmic tale is ever evolving, and these reflections guide us as we continue to write the story of algorithms in the pages of human history. With these insights, you're equipped to navigate, question, and contribute to the ongoing algorithmic narrative, making your mark on the digital landscape.

The Algorithmic Ecosystem: Balancing Nature and Innovation

Introduction: Harmony in the Digital Ecosystem

In this section, we delve into the realm of algorithms, likening it to a sprawling ecosystem. Much like the intricate balances found in nature, the universe of algorithms also demands a state of equilibrium. We will explore the interplay between algorithms, society, and the natural environment, examining ways to foster a symbiotic relationship that supports both technological advancement and the health of our digital world.

The Algorithmic Web: 'Interconnected Threads'

Picture algorithms as countless threads intricately woven into an immense digital tapestry. In this section, we're carefully unraveling the complex network of relationships that exist among these algorithms. We'll examine the way search algorithms determine our online discoveries and how recommendation systems are interconnected, providing insight into the elaborate ballet of algorithms that choreograph our digital experiences.

Example: Echo Chambers and Algorithmic Echoes

Ever noticed your online content becoming more and more aligned with your existing beliefs? We're uncovering the phenomenon of echo chambers, where algorithms amplify our preconceived notions. By understanding how these algorithmic echoes form, we're taking a step toward fostering diverse perspectives and breaking free from the confines of self-reinforcing information loops.

Society's Reflection: Algorithms and Cultural Impact

From algorithmic biases that perpetuate inequality to the potential for algorithms to drive social change, we're delving into the dynamic relationship between algorithms and society. By analyzing the role algorithms play in shaping cultural narratives, we're empowering ourselves to guide their influence responsibly.

Imagine algorithms inadvertently perpetuating social biases present in the data they're trained on. We're exploring algorithmic bias, its origins, and its far-reaching consequences. By understanding how algorithms can unintentionally amplify societal inequalities, we're advocating for ethical algorithmic design that promotes fairness and inclusivity.

Nature's Partner: Algorithms in Environmental Sustainability

Just as ecosystems rely on harmony to thrive, we're exploring how algorithms can contribute to environmental sustainability. From optimizing energy consumption to predicting natural disasters, we're uncovering the ways algorithms can play a vital role in protecting and preserving our planet. By harnessing algorithmic insights, we're working toward a future where technology and nature coexist harmoniously.

Imagine algorithms simulating climate patterns and helping us make informed decisions to mitigate climate change. We're delving into climate modeling, where algorithms use vast amounts of data to predict and understand environmental changes. Through this example, we're highlighting how algorithms become allies in the fight against climate crisis, paving the way for a greener, more sustainable world.

Balancing Act: Nurturing the Algorithmic Ecosystem

As we conclude this exploration of the algorithmic ecosystem, it's time to reflect on the importance of balance. From interconnected algorithms to their cultural and environmental impacts, we've witnessed the complex relationships that define this digital landscape. Remember, just as ecosystems thrive when they're nurtured, the algorithmic ecosystem requires our mindful stewardship. With the knowledge gained from this journey, you're now equipped to navigate this intricate web with a sense of responsibility, ensuring a harmonious coexistence between algorithmic innovation and the well-being of our digital and natural worlds.

The Human Algorithm Connection: Navigating Identity and Autonomy

Introduction: The Human Algorithm Nexus

In this penultimate section, we're diving deep into the intimate connection between humans and algorithms. Just as an intricate dance unfolds between partners, we're exploring the intricate dance between our human identities and the algorithms that shape our lives. From the realms of identity to the pursuit of autonomy, get ready to navigate the complex bond that defines the human-algorithm relationship.

Algorithmic Identity: Shaping Who We Are

Imagine algorithms as mirrors reflecting facets of our identity. In this part, we're delving into how algorithms influence our sense of self. From personalized ads that shape our preferences to algorithms that filter our social media feeds, we're unraveling how these digital companions craft an image of who we are in the virtual realm.

Ever scrolled through your social media feed and felt like the content resonated perfectly with your interests? We're exploring the phenomenon of algorithmic personalization, where our digital experiences echo and reinforce our identities. Through this lens, we're reflecting on how algorithms can both validate and challenge our self-perceptions.

Autonomy in the Algorithmic Era: Navigating Digital Sovereignty

From the choices we make to the information we consume; we're pondering how algorithms impact our ability to make independent decisions. By evaluating the balance between algorithmic assistance and personal sovereignty, we're empowering ourselves to navigate the digital landscape with agency.

Imagine algorithms tailoring your news feeds, showing you content aligned with your existing views. We're delving into the implications of this filtered reality, where exposure to diverse perspectives becomes limited. Through this example, we're reflecting on the importance of cultivating digital autonomy and seeking out information beyond algorithmic boundaries.

The Dance of Control: Managing the Human-Algorithm Partnership

As we explore the interplay between identity and autonomy, we must also address the balance of control in the human-algorithm partnership. In this section, we're reflecting on how much control we should cede to algorithms and how much agency we should retain. By examining the boundaries of this partnership, we're crafting a roadmap for a healthy, empowered relationship with algorithms.

Imagine letting algorithms guide your choices to discover new experiences. We're diving into the concept of algorithmic serendipity, where algorithms curate recommendations that introduce us to unexpected delights. Through this lens, we're contemplating how much control we're comfortable relinquishing to algorithms while maintaining our ability to embrace the joy of the unexpected.

Conclusion: The Harmony of Self and System

As we conclude this exploration of the human-algorithm connection, it's time to reflect on the intricate symphony that emerges from this partnership. From identity shaping to autonomy seeking, we've journeyed through the nuanced dynamics that define our interaction with algorithms. Remember, just as a dance requires synchronization, the human-algorithm connection thrives when we actively engage, assert our autonomy, and shape our digital identities. With these insights, you're poised to navigate the rhythm of this evolving relationship, embracing the harmony that emerges when human and algorithm unite.

Reflections on the Algorithmic Odyssey: Lessons and Legacy

A Moment of Contemplation

In this section, we pause to reflect on the monumental journey we've undertaken through the world of algorithms. Like a traveler returning home after an epic voyage, we're taking a moment to distill the wisdom gained from this odyssey. From the threads of knowledge woven through each part to the impact on our perceptions and actions, we're contemplating the lessons learned and the legacy we leave behind.

Unveiling Algorithmic Wisdom:

Key Takeaways

Imagine distilling the essence of our algorithmic expedition into a few key takeaways. In this part, we're unveiling the gems of wisdom acquired along the way. From understanding algorithms' power to shape our digital experiences to recognizing the ethical implications they pose; we're summarizing the core lessons that illuminate our path in the algorithmic landscape.

Imagine adopting an algorithmic mindset that embraces curiosity, adaptability, and ethical consideration. We're reflecting on the importance of cultivating this mindset, allowing us to navigate the evolving digital realm with confidence and awareness. By internalizing the lessons learned, we're shaping an approach that empowers us to thrive amidst the algorithmic tapestry.

The Footprints of Impact: Tracing Our Influence

Let us trace the footprints we've left behind as explorers in the algorithmic realm. Just as pioneers leave trails for others to follow, we're examining the ways our understanding of algorithms has impacted our digital interactions, ethical considerations, and technological choices. By recognizing our influence, we're acknowledging the mark we've made on the algorithmic landscape.

Imagine a digital world where citizens are informed, discerning, and proactive. We're reflecting on the transformation from passive consumers to empowered participants in the algorithmic ecosystem. By making conscious choices about our digital interactions and advocating for ethical algorithmic practices, we're leaving footprints that inspire others to follow suit.

The Legacy of Curiosity: Paving the Way Forward

As we conclude this algorithmic odyssey, we're contemplating the legacy we're leaving for future explorers of this ever-evolving landscape. Just as ancient explorers paved the way for generations to come, we're crafting a legacy of curiosity, responsibility, and a commitment to ethical algorithmic innovation. With this legacy, we're charting a course for a digital future that respects humanity's values and aspirations.

Imagine a legacy where ethical considerations are at the forefront of technological advancement. We're reflecting on the role we play as stewards of the algorithmic frontier, inspiring a culture that prioritizes ethical guidelines, safeguards against biases, and embraces the potential of algorithms to enhance our lives. By embodying this legacy, we're paving a path for a digital world that reflects our shared humanity.

Conclusion: Embarking on New Journeys

As we conclude this reflective journey through the world of algorithms, it's time to embrace the opportunities that lie ahead.

Just as this odyssey has deepened our understanding, the future beckons with new challenges and discoveries. Remember, the algorithmic odyssey is ongoing, and with the lessons learned, the legacy built, and the curiosity kindled, you're ready to embark on new journeys that shape the digital landscape for generations to come.

Algorithmic First Exercises

Welcome to the Algorithmic First Exercises—a collection of interactive journeys that delve into the intricate interplay between data-driven algorithms and the timeless power of human connection. Just as a symphony requires each instrument to play its part to create a harmonious melody, these exercises guide you through orchestrating personalized experiences that resonate with your audience.

We've now explored how algorithms compose personalized narratives, predict customer needs, and harmonize context and emotion. Now, with these exercises, it's your turn to step into the shoes of an algorithmic composer and craft experiences that leave lasting impressions. These exercises bridge the gap between theory and practice, enabling you to harness the potential of Algorithmic First in your brand's symphony.

Engage in hands-on activities to harmonize data-driven insights with your brand's symphony of customer experiences. These exercises provide a practical way to put the concepts explored in this part into action, fostering deeper connections between algorithms and your audience.

From crafting personalized preludes to orchestrating ethical compositions, these exercises empower you to conduct your brand's algorithmic orchestra with finesse. Dive into the interactive exercises to discover how Algorithmic First can elevate your brand's engagement and resonate with your audience on a whole new level.

As you embark on this journey, remember that Algorithmic First isn't just about data—it's about infusing personalization with empathy, ethics, and authenticity. Each exercise encourages you to reflect on the nuances of personalized experiences, respecting privacy, nurturing emotional connections, and aligning with your brand's values. Together, we'll craft experiences that resonate like a well-composed symphony, striking the perfect chords between data and human touch. So, let's dive in and start composing experiences that sing with the harmony of Algorithmic First.

Exercise 1: Algorithmic Deconstruction

Objective: To understand the components and processes behind algorithms

Instructions:

1. Choose a simple everyday task, such as making a sandwich or getting dressed.

2. Break down the task into smaller steps and decisions.

3. Identify the logical sequence of these steps and decisions.

4. Imagine you're creating an algorithm for this task. Write down the sequence of steps and decisions in a clear, concise manner.

5. Reflect on how you've broken down the task and compare it to the way algorithms process data.

Exercise 2: Algorithmic Analysis

Objective: To analyze the impact of algorithms on digital experiences.

Instructions:

1. Pick an online platform or service you frequently use, such as a social media app or an e-commerce website.

2. Identify the key areas where algorithms play a role, such as recommendations, search results, or personalized content.

3. Document the different ways algorithms tailor your experience on this platform.

4. Consider how your interactions might differ without algorithmic influence.

5. Reflect on how algorithms shape your digital experience and whether you find it beneficial or limiting.

Exercise 3: Ethical Algorithm Exploration

Objective: To examine the ethical considerations associated with algorithms.

Instructions:

1. Choose a controversial topic, such as political news or health information.

2. Conduct a search on a search engine or social media platform using relevant keywords.

3. Observe the content and sources that appear in the search results.

4. Analyze whether there's a bias or skew in the information presented.

5. Reflect on the ethical implications of algorithmic biases and their potential impact on public perception.

Exercise 4: Algorithmic Personalization Audit

Objective: To evaluate the extent of algorithmic personalization in your online interactions.

Instructions:

1. Visit your favorite e-commerce website or streaming service.

2. Explore various sections, such as recommended products, playlists, or movie suggestions.

3. Compare these recommendations to your preferences and previous interactions on the platform.

4. Reflect on the accuracy of the algorithm's suggestions and whether they align with your interests.

5. Consider the benefits and drawbacks of algorithmic personalization for your experience.

Exercise 5: Algorithmic Future Visualization

Objective: To envision the potential future of algorithms in your daily life.

Instructions:

1. Select a scenario from your daily routine, like commuting to work, cooking, or shopping.

2. Imagine how algorithms could enhance or alter this scenario in the next 10 years.

3. Visualize the changes in efficiency, convenience, and personalization.

4. Consider both positive and negative impacts of increased algorithmic integration.

5. Reflect on your vision and discuss with others to explore different perspectives on the future of algorithms.

Exercise 6: Algorithmic Collaborative Creation

Objective: To experience the synergy between human creativity and algorithmic assistance.

Instructions:

1. Choose a creative project, such as writing a short story, composing a piece of music, or creating digital artwork.

2. Start working on the project, making deliberate creative decisions.

3. Introduce an algorithmic element, such as using a random word generator for story prompts, an AI music composer, or a filter for image manipulation.

4. Incorporate the algorithmic suggestions into your project and observe the impact on your creative process.

5. Reflect on how the collaboration between your creativity and the algorithmic tool influenced the outcome and your experience.

Exercise 7: Algorithmic Bias Awareness

Objective: To recognize and address potential biases in algorithmic systems.

Instructions:

1. Choose a popular online search engine or social media platform.

2. Search for a few topics related to sensitive subjects, such as gender, race, or political affiliations.

3. Take note of the content that appears in the search results or your feed.

4. Analyze whether the algorithmic system shows any bias or favoritism toward certain perspectives.

5. Reflect on the implications of algorithmic bias for shaping public opinion and consider ways to address or mitigate these biases.

Exercise 8: Algorithmic Forecasting

Objective: To predict trends and patterns using algorithmic thinking.

Instructions:

1. Select a topic of interest, such as fashion, technology, or entertainment.

2. Gather data from various sources related to your chosen topic (news articles, social media trends, etc.).

3. Identify recurring patterns and trends within the data.

4. Use your observations to make predictions about potential future developments in the chosen domain.

5. Reflect on the accuracy of your predictions and the role of algorithms in identifying patterns that shape trends.

Exercise 9: Algorithmic Artistry

Objective: To explore the creative potential of algorithm-generated art.

Instructions:

1. Research algorithms that generate visual art, such as the "DeepDream" algorithm or generative adversarial networks (GANs).

2. Experiment with an online tool or software that utilizes algorithmic art creation.

3. Allow the algorithm to generate visual content based on parameters you set.

4. Observe the unique patterns and designs the algorithm produces.

5. Reflect on the collaboration between algorithmic processes and artistic expression, considering the boundaries of creativity in algorithm-generated art.

Exercise 10: Ethical Algorithm Design

Objective: To engage in designing an algorithm with ethical considerations.

Instructions:

1. Choose a scenario where an algorithm could have a significant impact, such as a healthcare diagnosis tool or a content recommendation system.

2. Brainstorm potential positive and negative consequences of the algorithm's decisions.

3. Design a framework that incorporates ethical considerations, transparency, and fairness into the algorithm's decision-making process.

4. Reflect on how your ethical framework aligns with responsible algorithm design and its potential impact on users or stakeholders.

5. Share your design and engage in discussions with peers to gather diverse perspectives on the ethical implications of your algorithmic approach.

Algorithmic Symphony: A Mental Model for Personalized Engagement

Prelude: Personalized Overture

Set the stage for a captivating engagement by tailoring the introduction to resonate with everyone.

Harmony in Context

Craft experiences that seamlessly adapt to various touchpoints, creating a harmonious symphony of relevance.

Emotion-Fueled Crescendos

Design journeys that build emotional connections, leading to powerful and memorable interactions.

Predictive Prelude

Anticipate customer actions and guide them towards desired outcomes, creating a predictive rhythm.

Orchestration of Habit Loops

Shape customer habits through customized suggestions, creating a rhythm that encourages ongoing engagement.

Serendipity in Melody

Create delightful surprises using anticipatory algorithms, infusing the melody with serendipitous moments.

The Composer's Craft

Explore the art of algorithmic composition, where algorithms act as composers, orchestrating personalized experiences.

Narrative Crescendo

Craft evolving narratives that unfold over time, enhancing engagement through dynamic storytelling.

Ethical Harmony

Examine the ethical considerations within algorithmic personalization, ensuring that responsible practices guide the composition.

Symphony of Serendipity

Weave serendipitous moments into customer journeys through algorithmic insights, enriching the symphonic experience.

Emotional Harmonies

Craft data-driven narratives that evoke emotions, transforming engagement into an emotionally resonant melody.

Resonance and Trust

Build trust by aligning algorithmic insights with customer values, creating a harmonious balance of resonance.

Algorithmic Composition

Orchestrate interactions that seamlessly blend data precision with emotional depth, creating an intricate symphony.

Creativity's Crescendo

Infuse creative flair into algorithmic strategies, making the symphony of engagement an artistic masterpiece.

Humanity's Melody

Balance data insights with a human touch, infusing authenticity into the symphonic experience.

Reflections and Refrains

Reflect on personal insights gained from Algorithmic Symphony, creating moments of introspection and growth.

Envisioning Future Crescendos

Envision the evolving role of algorithms and personalization in shaping the future of engaging experiences, creating a harmonious symphony that continues to resonate.

Epilogue: The Infinite Algorithmic Horizon

In this final epilogue, we stand at the precipice of the infinite algorithmic horizon. Having journeyed through the diverse landscapes of algorithms, reflections, and impacts, we find ourselves on the threshold of what lies beyond. From the grand tapestry of perspectives to the echoes of ethical considerations, our odyssey has equipped us with insights that resonate far into the future.

The Uncharted Beyond: A Continual Exploration

As we gaze into the uncharted beyond, we recognize that our algorithmic journey is perpetual. Just as explorers of old set sail to uncover new continents, we too are poised to explore the ever-expanding frontiers of algorithms. With the power of innovation and the torch of ethical awareness, we embark on a journey that continually reshapes the boundaries of human potential.

The Symphony of Humanity and Algorithms: A Harmonious Future

Our odyssey has revealed the intricate symphony that emerges from the interplay between humanity and algorithms. Like skilled conductors, we have the power to shape the melodies of this symphony, ensuring that the notes of progress, inclusivity, and respect harmonize with the rhythms of innovation. As we move forward, let us remember that the future is a shared composition, where humans and algorithms dance in harmonious partnership.

Embracing the Algorithmic Epoch: Crafting a Legacy

Just as epochs mark distinct periods in history, our algorithmic epoch is defined by collaboration, empowerment, and ethical consciousness. We have the privilege to shape this epoch's legacy, leaving behind a tapestry woven with wisdom, empathy, and innovation. Let us inspire future generations to approach algorithms with a sense of wonder, a commitment to ethics, and a determination to amplify human flourishing.

Closing the Part: A Prelude to New Beginnings

And so, as we close the part on this algorithmic odyssey, we recognize that endings are but preludes to new beginnings. Our journey through algorithms, from their mysteries to their impacts, has given us a lens through which to view the ever-evolving landscape of technology. Armed with insights, we're prepared to embrace the next part, crafting experiences that honor our shared humanity and chart a course toward a future shaped by the symphony of human and algorithmic potential. As we continue forward, may the symphony of innovation, ethics, and imagination guide our way into the boundless possibilities of the algorithmic horizon.

Reflections

Strategic Scalers: Crafting a Unique AI Strategy

Distinctive Strategy	Description and Analogy
1. The "Intentional" AI Drive	Strategic Scalers approach AI with intentionality, ensuring every initiative has a clear purpose. **Analogy**: Like conductors of an orchestra, they create AI symphonies with precise intent.
2. The Art of Tuning Out Data Noise	They possess the skill to filter out irrelevant data, focusing on what truly matters in AI-driven decisions. **Analogy**: Like seasoned sommeliers, they distinguish fine wine from vinegar in the data sea.
3. Collaborative Sport	Recognizing AI's collaborative nature, they form cross-functional teams, blending AI and non-AI expertise. **Analogy**: They are architects of collaboration, constructing teams where talents harmoniously merge, like a well-coordinated ensemble.

Algorithms Can Make Your Organization Self-Tuning

Key Insights	Description
1. The "Self-Tuning Enterprise"	- Ming Zeng of Alibaba introduced the concept of the "self-tuning enterprise." - The idea is to let market mechanisms manage what is better left to them.
2. Bringing the Marketplace Inside	- Alibaba aimed to not only institutionalize change but also integrate the marketplace into the organization. - Continuous updates were applied to product offerings, vision, business model, organization, and information systems.
3. Multi-Armed Bandit Algorithms	- The effectiveness of different approaches to strategy and execution was modeled using multi-armed bandit algorithms. - These algorithms are excellent at rapidly adapting to changing customer needs.
4. Principles for a Self-Tuning Enterprise	- The goal is to replace fixed or top-down elements of a company's business system with self-directed mechanisms that continuously evolve based on and shape the marketplace.
5. Algorithmic Thinking in Business	- Algorithmic competition is becoming increasingly important in business. It involves updating key business concepts like vision, organization, business model, and information systems in complex and dynamic environments.

PART-4

NARRATIVES

MASTERING THE ART OF STORYTELLING

Mastering the Art of Storytelling

Introduction: Crafting Stories That Resonate

In today's dynamic world of branding, brands have transformed into platforms for significant engagement, not just mere products. With the shift in revenue models favoring subscriptions and algorithm-driven strategies, the role of proficient communication is paramount. We delve further into the essence of branding's remarkable ability to change and influence.

Having explored the concepts of brand-as-a-platform, revenue subscribed, and algorithmic-first approaches, we now delve into a dimension that binds these ideas together into a cohesive whole—the art of storytelling. Just as algorithms optimize and subscriptions create committed relationships, narratives form the emotional threads that tie customers to brands in a profound and lasting manner.

In this segment, we invite you to embark on an exploration of how storytelling takes center stage in the modern art of branding. From understanding the narrative threads that weave through brand ecosystems to discovering the symphony of stories that resonate across diverse touchpoints, we unravel the nuances of the "Narrative Way."

As we journey deeper, you will see how narratives amplify brand identity, engage diverse audiences, and transcend cultural boundaries. These narratives become the bridges that connect brand values to customer emotions, resulting in a resonance that leaves a lasting imprint. You will witness how narratives are not only tools of communication but also the foundation of authenticity, ethics, and empathy in a brand's voice.

This segment builds upon the concepts explored in earlier parts, adding a new layer of depth and dimension to the evolving landscape of branding. Just as a brand platform offers a stage for narratives to unfold, and subscription models establish a commitment to ongoing engagement, narratives are the enchanting melodies that captivate hearts and minds.

Imagine a world where every brand interaction is a story—a captivating narrative that draws customers in, engages their emotions, and leaves a lasting impression. Welcome to the realm of the "Narrative Way," where storytelling takes center stage in the art of branding. Just as a skilled storyteller weaves words to create a vivid tapestry, brands can use narratives to create memorable experiences that resonate deeply.

Join us in discovering the transformative power of narratives— the threads that weave cultures, the bridges that connect diverse perspectives, and the echoes that reverberate through time. As we explore the importance of "Narratives" you'll uncover how crafting stories that resonate isn't just about communication; it's about creating experiences that leave an indelible legacy.

The Storyteller's Palette

Painting with Words

Much like a painter uses colors to evoke emotions, storytellers use words to craft narratives that resonate. In this section, we'll examine the elements that make up a compelling brand narrative. Just as a painter selects the right hues, storytellers choose words that create vivid imagery and transport audiences into the heart of the story.

Metaphors and Analogies: Words as Brushstrokes

Words are the brushstrokes that paint the canvas of a brand's narrative. Just as an artist layers colors to create depth, storytellers layer words to build a rich and immersive narrative that captivates the audience. Each word is a deliberate choice, contributing to the overall composition of the story.

Just as a skilled painter layers colors to create depth and dimension on a canvas, storytellers' layer carefully chosen words to construct intricate narratives. Consider the way a luxury fashion brand describes their products: "Each stitch is a brushstroke, and every fabric choice contributes to the masterpiece we create for you."

Contrasting Perspectives: The Balance of Fact and Emotion

Every narrative strikes a balance between information and emotional resonance. Just as a painting combines realism with interpretation, brand narratives intertwine facts and emotions to create a holistic and impactful experience. Explore how different brands master this balance to tell stories that engage both the mind and the heart.

Imagine a tech company launching a new product. Their narrative seamlessly blends the technical specifications (facts) with the excitement and anticipation that customers feel (emotion). Through this balance, they create a narrative that not only informs but also engages customers on a personal level.

From Characters to Customers

Characters as Archetypes

Characters in a story mirror archetype that audiences recognize and connect with. Similarly, brands can create customer personas that embody these archetypes, allowing customers to see themselves in the narrative. Dive into how brands can transform customers into protagonists, making them central to the narrative's unfolding.

Metaphors and Analogies: Brands as Co-Stars

Just as characters in a story have their arcs and journeys, brands can become co-stars in the narratives they weave. Brands take on roles that complement the customer's journey, guiding them through challenges and triumphs. Explore how brands can become integral to customers' personal stories, creating a sense of belonging and shared experiences.

Just as a protagonist's journey is enriched by supporting characters, a brand can play a vital role in the customer's journey. Think of an outdoor adventure brand that positions itself as the customer's guide, embarking on a journey together, facing challenges and experiencing triumphs side by side.

Human Touch: Empathy and Relatability

Empathy is the bridge that connects characters to readers, and brands can leverage the same connection with customers. Just as readers empathize with fictional characters, customers empathize with brands that demonstrate an understanding of their needs and aspirations. Discover how brands can infuse empathy into their narratives, fostering deeper connections.

Consider a skincare brand that understands the struggles of its customers. They share stories of individuals who faced similar skin issues, conveying empathy and relatability. By showing genuine understanding, the brand deepens its connection with customers and becomes a partner in their journey towards healthier skin.

The Arc of Engagement

Unfolding Narratives

Narratives are defined by their arcs—how they build tension, reach climaxes, and resolve conflicts. In branding, narratives can mirror the customer journey, from awareness to loyalty. Just as stories keep readers engaged, brand narratives keep customers captivated across every touchpoint.

Metaphors and Analogies: Brand Journeys as Quests

Just as a hero overcomes obstacles on a quest, a fitness brand can frame a customer's fitness journey as a heroic quest. They guide customers through challenges, celebrating milestones as triumphs. This narrative structure enhances the sense of achievement and engagement throughout the fitness journey.

A brand's journey can parallel the hero's journey—a classic narrative archetype. Brands guide customers through quests that lead to personal growth and transformation. Explore how brands can structure their narratives to align with the stages of a customer's journey, creating narratives that resonate with the path to success.

Reflective Closure: Resonance and Impact

Reflect on how a nostalgic video game company evokes strong emotions through its storytelling. The closure could emphasize how these narratives not only shape the perception of the brand but also create a community of loyal fans who share a common emotional connection.

Just as a powerful ending lingers in readers' minds, impactful brand narratives leave a lasting impression. Reflect on how narratives influence brand perception, customer loyalty, and emotional resonance. Sum up the section's insights, emphasizing the importance of crafting narratives that leave customers inspired and connected.

The Power of Symbols

Symbols as Story Anchors

Symbols hold profound meaning in both stories and brands. In this section, we'll explore how symbols can become anchors that connect customers to the core narrative. Just as symbols carry cultural significance in stories, brands can use symbols to evoke emotions and communicate values, creating a shared language with their audience.

Metaphors and Analogies: Symbols as Threads

Imagine a coffee company using a simple coffee cup symbol across all its products and marketing materials. Just as a recurring motif binds a story together, this symbol reinforces the brand's identity and mission, creating a cohesive and recognizable narrative for customers.

Symbols thread through the fabric of a narrative, weaving a tapestry of meaning and emotion. Just as symbols recur in stories, they recur in brand narratives, creating a consistent thread that reinforces brand identity. Delve into how brands can select and utilize symbols to create a coherent and memorable narrative.

Contrasting Perspectives: Multilayered Symbolism

Consider an eco-conscious fashion brand that incorporates leaves as symbols. These leaves represent environmental sustainability, growth, and renewal. Delve into how these symbols resonate differently with various customer segments, providing a layered narrative experience.

Symbols often hold multiple layers of meaning, enriching the narrative experience. Just as literary symbols carry hidden significance, brand symbols can hold deeper meanings that resonate with different customer segments. Examine how brands can employ multilayered symbolism to engage diverse audiences on various levels.

Storytelling Through Visuals

Visual Narratives

Storytelling isn't limited to words; visuals also play a vital role in conveying narratives. In this section, we'll uncover how visual elements—such as design, color, and imagery—contribute to the overall brand narrative. Just as a story's setting creates atmosphere, visuals shape the backdrop against which the brand narrative unfolds.

Metaphors and Analogies: Visuals as Brushstrokes

Visual elements are the brushstrokes that paint the visual narrative of a brand. Just as artists use brushstrokes to convey emotions, designers use visuals to evoke feelings and enhance the brand story. Explore how visual storytelling adds depth and layers to the narrative experience.

Imagine an art-themed brand that uses a palette of vibrant colors and bold strokes in its visuals to convey creativity and passion, adding depth to the brand's story.

Human Touch: Visual Storytelling and Emotion

Visuals have the power to evoke emotions that words alone might struggle to express. Just as characters' facial expressions convey emotions in stories, visuals can communicate brand values and emotions to customers. Discover how brands can create emotionally resonant visual narratives that connect on a visceral level.

A luxury car brand might use sleek and elegant visuals to evoke a sense of sophistication and aspiration. Just as characters' facial expressions convey emotions in stories, these visuals can elicit emotions that resonate with customers' desires and aspirations.

A Symphony of Stories

Narrative Ecosystems

Brands have a multitude of narratives, each contributing to the overall brand ecosystem. In this section, we'll delve into how various narratives—from brand origin stories to customer testimonials—interact and form a symphony of stories. Just as a symphony comprises diverse instruments, brand narratives harmonize to create a holistic brand experience.

Metaphors and Analogies: Narratives as Harmonies

Each narrative is a harmony that adds depth and texture to the brand's symphony. Just as harmonies enrich a musical piece, narratives enrich the brand experience by providing diverse perspectives and angles. Explore how to orchestrate a symphony of narratives that resonate with different customer segments.

Think of a food brand that weaves together narratives of its ingredients' origins, its chefs' expertise, and customers' experiences. Just as harmonies create a richer musical experience, these narratives blend to create a multi-dimensional brand experience that resonates with diverse customers.

Reflective Closure: Storytelling Resonance

As a story's impact lingers beyond its last page, brand narratives leave a lasting imprint. Reflect on the resonance that storytelling creates—how narratives shape brand identity, build emotional connections, and foster customer loyalty. Sum up the section's insights, emphasizing the significance of crafting narratives that echo in the hearts of customers.

Reflect on how a global technology brand's diverse narrative—ranging from user success stories to the brand's evolution over time—form a symphony of narratives that enrich the brand's identity and deepen its customer connections.

Narrative Alchemy: Transformative Branding

The Alchemical Process

Much like an alchemist transforms base materials into gold, brands can use narratives to transform their essence into something extraordinary. In this section, we'll delve into the alchemy of narrative branding—how stories can elevate brands from ordinary to remarkable. Just as alchemy seeks to create a higher form, narrative alchemy elevates brand perception and value through storytelling.

Metaphors and Analogies: Brand Transformation as Alchemy

Just as alchemy seeks to transmute elements, brands can transmute their image through compelling narratives. Narratives are the catalysts that turn brand experiences into golden moments of connection. Explore how brands can leverage storytelling to reshape perceptions and establish a profound emotional bond.

Imagine a struggling retail brand that transforms its image through a heartfelt narrative. Just as alchemical processes change the essence of materials, this narrative alchemy elevates the brand from a struggling entity to a beloved and transformed symbol of resilience.

Contrasting Perspectives: The Elixir of Authenticity

Authenticity is the elixir that gives narratives their potency. Just as alchemical elixirs promise transformation, authentic brand narratives promise genuine value. Examine how brands can maintain authenticity while using storytelling as a tool for transformation, striking the balance between enchantment and truth.

Consider a fast-food chain that embraces its roots while evolving its narrative to align with changing customer preferences. Just as alchemical elixirs promise transformation, this brand's authentic narrative promises genuine value, striking a balance between nostalgic charm and modern relevance.

Echoes Across Time: Enduring Narratives

The Echoes of Time

A well-crafted narrative can resonate through generations, leaving an everlasting impact. In this section, we'll explore how enduring narratives become part of cultural consciousness, much like timeless stories passed down through ages. Just as echoes linger in the air, enduring narratives linger in the minds and hearts of audiences.

Metaphors and Analogies: Narratives as Time Travelers

Narratives are like time travelers, transcending eras to leave an indelible mark on society. Just as classic tales inspire new adaptations, enduring brand narratives inspire ongoing relevance and evolution. Discover how brands can craft narratives that stand the test of time and remain relevant in an ever-changing landscape.

Imagine a luxury watch brand that tells stories of craftsmanship passed down through generations. Just as enduring tales inspire new adaptations, these narratives inspire the brand's ongoing relevance, connecting the past with the present.

Reflective Closure: Legacy in Narratives

Just as legacies are the footprints of history, narratives leave behind a brand's legacy. Reflect on the significance of crafting narratives that contribute to a brand's lasting impact. Sum up the section's insights, emphasizing the role of enduring narratives in creating a brand's place in history.

Reflect on how an iconic beverage brand's enduring narrative of celebration, friendship, and enjoyment has transcended time, became a part of cultural consciousness and leaving an indelible legacy in the hearts of customers.

The Narrator's Call

The Art of Delivery

Just as a skilled narrator captivates listeners with their delivery, brands can captivate customers with their storytelling approach. In this section, we'll explore how the delivery of narratives—across different channels and mediums—shapes the overall brand experience. Just as a narrator sets the tone, brands set the tone for customer interactions through narrative delivery.

Metaphors and Analogies: Brand as Narrator

A brand becomes the narrator of its own story, using different mediums to engage audiences. Just as a skilled narrator adapts their tone to suit the story's mood, brands adapt their narrative delivery to match the context and customer expectations. Dive into how brands can effectively narrate their stories across various touchpoints.

Think of a travel company that narrates its customers' journeys through captivating videos, blog posts, and social media updates. Just as a narrator adapts their tone to the story's mood, the brand adapts its narrative delivery to match the unique aspects of each customer's travel experience.

Human Touch: Authentic Narration

Authenticity in narration ensures a genuine connection with the audience. Just as listeners connect with sincere narrators, customers connect with brands that tell their stories with honesty and transparency. Explore how brands can infuse their narratives with an authentic voice, fostering trust and forging stronger relationships.

Consider a sustainability-focused brand that narrates its commitment to environmental causes with sincerity and transparency. Just as listeners connect with authentic narrators, customers connect with brands that genuinely communicate their values and principles.

The Resonance of Narratives

Much like a well-told story echoes in the mind, the narratives brands craft echo in the hearts of customers. As we conclude our journey through this segment, consider the power of narratives to shape perceptions, evoke emotions, and foster lasting connections. Just as a memorable story is retold through generations, the narratives you create today can leave a legacy that reverberates through time.

Crafting the Story Ecosystem

The Narrative Network

Stories are interconnected, creating a narrative ecosystem that encompasses a brand's essence. In this section, we'll explore how brands can weave a network of narratives—each contributing to the overarching brand story. Just as ecosystems support diverse life forms, brand narratives support diverse interactions, forming a comprehensive experience.

Metaphors and Analogies: Brand Narratives as Ecosystem Threads

Narratives are the threads that weave through the brand ecosystem, connecting touchpoints and interactions. Just as ecosystems thrive on diversity, brand narratives thrive on multiplicity, offering customers various entry points and engagement opportunities. Delve into how brands can cultivate a rich narrative ecosystem that caters to diverse audience needs.

Imagine a tech company crafting a narrative ecosystem that includes origin stories, customer testimonials, and innovation showcases. Just as ecosystems thrive on diversity, this narrative ecosystem supports a range of interactions, providing a comprehensive brand experience.

Contrasting Perspectives: Symbiotic Storytelling

In ecosystems, different species form symbiotic relationships for mutual benefit. Similarly, brand narratives can interconnect to enhance each other's impact. Examine how brands can strategically link narratives, creating a symbiotic relationship where one narrative enhances the resonance and relevance of another.

Consider how a lifestyle brand's narratives about community engagement and philanthropy mutually enhance each other. Just as species form symbiotic relationships in ecosystems, these narratives interconnect to amplify each other's impact and relevance.

The Storytelling Lens in Design

Designing with Stories

Design and storytelling share a symbiotic relationship, each enhancing the other's impact. In this section, we'll uncover how design elements can amplify brand narratives, turning stories into visual and experiential journeys. Just as a lens focuses light, design focuses narratives to create compelling brand experiences.

Metaphors and Analogies: Design as Narrative Amplifier

Design elements are the amplifiers that project the brand's narrative to audiences. Just as a magnifying glass intensifies light, design intensifies the emotions and messages conveyed by narratives. Explore how design choices—from typography to layout—can enhance the narrative's resonance and emotional impact.

Consider a high-end jewelry brand that uses intricate design elements to amplify its narrative. Just as a jeweler carefully selects and places precious gemstones to create a dazzling masterpiece, the brand's designers meticulously choose colors, fonts, and layouts to enhance the storytelling experience. The design elements serve as the setting that showcases the brand's narrative, elevating the emotions and messages behind each piece of jewelry.

Reflective Closure: Designing Emotionally Resonant Narratives

Just as the right camera lens captures emotion in a photograph, the right design lens captures emotion in brand narratives. Reflect on the significance of design in storytelling, emphasizing the role of visual elements in conveying emotions and enhancing the brand experience.

Reflect on the parallel between a skilled photographer choosing the perfect lens to capture raw emotion and a brand's design team selecting the right visual elements to evoke emotions in narratives. Just as the camera lens brings focus and depth to a photograph, the design lens brings focus and depth to brand narratives. Acknowledge the role of design in creating emotionally resonant narratives, emphasizing how visual elements play a pivotal role in conveying emotions and intensifying the impact of the brand experience.

The Digital Chronicle

Narratives in the Digital Age

In the digital landscape, narratives take on new dimensions, reshaping the way brands engage with audiences. In this section, we'll explore how digital platforms amplify narratives and enable brands to create immersive, interactive experiences. Just as a chronicle documents history, the digital realm documents brand stories for a global audience.

Metaphors and Analogies: Digital Platforms as Story Portals

Digital platforms are the portals that transport audiences into brand narratives. Just as portals connect different realms, digital platforms connect brands with diverse audiences worldwide. Discover how brands can leverage digital tools—from social media to immersive websites—to share their narratives on a global scale.

Imagine digital platforms as magical portals that transport audiences into the captivating worlds of brand narratives. Just as portals bridge different realms, digital platforms bridge the physical and virtual spaces, connecting brands with audiences from all corners of the globe. These platforms serve as gateways to immersive experiences, allowing brands to invite customers to step into their stories and engage with their narratives on a global scale.

Human Touch: Authenticity in the Digital Age

In the digital realm, authenticity remains a cornerstone of effective storytelling. Just as authenticity fosters trust in personal interactions, digital authenticity fosters trust between brands and customers. Explore how brands can maintain a genuine voice in their digital narratives, creating meaningful connections across screens.

Consider the analogy of a warm, authentic conversation between friends that fosters trust and connection. Just as authenticity is crucial in personal interactions, it remains vital in the digital realm. Brands must maintain an honest and genuine voice in their digital narratives, creating a sense of transparency that resonates with customers. Just as people value real connections, customers value authentic brands in the digital age. Explore how brands can uphold authenticity in their digital storytelling, forging meaningful connections across screens and devices.

The Legacy of Narratives

Just as stories leave an imprint on culture, brand narratives leave an imprint on customer perceptions. As you conclude your exploration of Part 4, "Narrative Way," carry with you the knowledge that narratives have the power to shape brand identity, evoke emotions, and foster deep connections. Just as a memorable story is retold through generations, the narratives you craft have the potential to create a lasting legacy that influences brand loyalty and resonance.

The Evolution of Narratives

Narrative Dynamics

Narratives are not static; they evolve with time and adapt to changing contexts. In this section, we'll examine how brand narratives can evolve to remain relevant and engaging in an ever-changing landscape. Just as stories take unexpected twists, brand narratives can pivot to capture new audiences and address evolving needs.

Metaphors and Analogies: Narratives as Living Organisms

Narratives are living entities that respond to their environment. Just as organisms adapt to survive, brand narratives can adapt to thrive in the dynamic market landscape. Explore how brands can infuse flexibility into their narratives, allowing them to grow and evolve with shifting trends and customer expectations.

Think of narratives as living organisms that interact and evolve with their surroundings. Just as organisms adapt to changes in their environment, brand narratives can adapt to changes in the market landscape. These narratives respond to shifting trends, customer behaviors, and cultural shifts, ensuring their relevance and resonance over time. Just as living organisms thrive through adaptation, brand narratives thrive by staying flexible and dynamic.

Contrasting Perspectives: Tradition and Innovation in Narratives

Tradition and innovation coexist in narratives, preserving core elements while embracing new ideas. Just as classical literature is reimagined in modern retellings, brand narratives can bridge the gap between tradition and innovation. Examine how brands can infuse fresh perspectives into established narratives, resonating with both traditionalists and modern audiences.

Consider how a classic fairy tale, such as Cinderella, remains beloved across generations while also inspiring new adaptations. Similarly, brand narratives can balance tradition and innovation. They can hold onto their core values and stories while embracing new ideas and approaches. This approach allows brands to resonate with both traditionalists who appreciate continuity and modern audiences who seek innovation. Explore how brands can weave the threads of tradition and innovation into their narratives, creating a narrative tapestry that captures the best of both worlds.

Immersive Story worlds

Building Narrative Universes

Immersive narratives create entire worlds that customers can step into. In this section, we'll explore how brands can construct narrative universes that envelop customers in engaging experiences. Just as authors create fictional worlds, brands can build immersive environments that draw customers into the heart of the narrative.

Metaphors and Analogies: Brand Worlds as Alternate Realities

Narrative universes are alternate realities where customers can explore and engage. Just as science fiction transports readers to distant galaxies, brand immersive experiences transport customers to unique story worlds. Delve into how brands can leverage technology—from virtual reality to interactive websites—to craft captivating narrative universes.

Imagine brand narrative universes as parallel dimensions, where customers can step into alternate realities and engage with captivating stories. Just as science fiction novels transport readers to distant galaxies, brand immersive experiences transport customers to unique and engaging story worlds. These story worlds provide an opportunity for customers to explore, interact, and connect with the brand's narratives in a deeply engaging way.

Reflective Closure: The Impact of Immersive Experiences

Just as readers remember the settings of their favorite books, customers remember the immersive experiences brands provide. Reflect on the significance of narrative universes in modern branding, emphasizing how immersive experiences create lasting memories and emotional connections.

Reflect on the way readers vividly remember the settings of their favorite books, and how customers similarly remember the immersive experiences provided by brands. Just as the worlds within stories stay with readers, the narrative universes crafted by brands through immersive experiences leave a lasting imprint on customers. Acknowledge the transformative impact of immersive experiences in modern branding, highlighting how these experiences not only create lasting memories but also forge emotional connections that resonate long after the interaction has ended.

Storytelling Across Cultures

Cultural Narratives

Narratives transcend cultural boundaries, connecting with audiences around the world. In this section, we'll explore how brands can craft narratives that resonate with diverse cultures and backgrounds. Just as myths and legends are shared across cultures, brand narratives can bridge cultural gaps and foster inclusivity.

Metaphors and Analogies: Narratives as Global Bridges

Narratives are bridges that unite diverse cultures under shared experiences. Just as ancient stories find relevance in contemporary times, brand narratives can draw inspiration from cultural legacies to create relatable and universal stories. Discover how brands can align their narratives with cultural values and create narratives that resonate globally.

Imagine narratives as bridges that span across diverse cultures, connecting people through shared experiences. Just as ancient stories continue to hold relevance in contemporary times, brand narratives can draw inspiration from cultural legacies, myths, and traditions to create stories that resonate universally. These narratives act as bridges that bring together individuals from different backgrounds under the umbrella of a shared narrative.

Human Touch: Sensitivity and Authenticity in Cross-Cultural Narratives

In cross-cultural narratives, sensitivity and authenticity are paramount. Just as cultural understanding builds bridges between people, cross-cultural narratives build bridges between brands and audiences. Explore how brands can navigate cultural nuances with respect and authenticity, fostering connections that transcend borders.

Consider the analogy of cultural understanding being the key to building bridges between people from different parts of the world. Just as cross-cultural sensitivity fosters connections between individuals, cross-cultural brand narratives foster connections between brands and global audiences. Brands can navigate cultural nuances with respect and authenticity, ensuring that their narratives resonate across borders without causing offense or misunderstanding. Explore how brands can approach cross-cultural storytelling with care, crafting narratives that celebrate diversity and foster connections that transcend geographical boundaries.

Beyond Words, Lasting Impact

Narratives transcend language; they evoke emotions and memories that linger long after they are heard. As you conclude your exploration of Part 4, "Narrative Way," remember that the stories you craft have the potential to transcend words and create lasting impact. Just as a moving story is retold through generations, the narratives you create have the power to shape brand perception, create emotional resonance, and inspire action.

The Dynamics of Dialogue

Conversational Narratives

Narratives extend beyond monologues; they thrive in dialogue and interaction. In this section, we'll delve into the dynamics of conversational narratives, where brands engage in meaningful conversations with their customers. Just as characters exchange dialogues in stories, brands can create narratives that evolve through customer interactions.

Metaphors and Analogies: Brands as Dialogue Partners

Brands become partners in dialogue, listening and responding to customers' voices. Just as characters engage in back-and-forth conversations, brands can establish a dialogue that fosters genuine connections. Explore how brands can leverage social media, chatbots, and other channels to create dynamic conversational narratives.

Imagine brands as partners in an ongoing dialogue, engaging in meaningful conversations with their customers. Just as characters in a story exchange thoughts and ideas, brands can establish a dynamic dialogue that encourages open communication and fosters genuine connections. This dialogue isn't one-sided but rather a two-way exchange that allows brands to listen and respond to customers' voices.

Reflective Closure: The Impact of Genuine Conversations

Just as a heartfelt conversation leaves a lasting impact, genuine brand conversations resonate with customers. Reflect on the significance of conversational narratives in building trust, fostering loyalty, and creating an open channel for customers to share their thoughts and feelings.

Reflect on the way heartfelt conversations leave a lasting impact on individuals, and how genuine brand conversations similarly resonate with customers. Just as authentic conversations build trust and strengthen relationships, genuine brand conversations play a pivotal role in building trust, fostering customer loyalty, and creating an open channel for customers to share their thoughts, feelings, and feedback. Acknowledge the power of conversational narratives in shaping brand-customer relationships, emphasizing their role in creating a strong foundation of mutual understanding and connection.

Storytelling Through Experiences

Experiential Narratives

Narratives unfold not only through words but also through experiences. In this section, we'll uncover how brands can use experiential elements to create immersive brand narratives. Just as readers step into the worlds of stories, customers can step into the worlds of brands through memorable experiences.

Metaphors and Analogies: Experiences as Narrative Spaces

Experiences become spaces where narratives come to life. Just as theater productions engage audiences through multisensory experiences, brands can stage memorable events that immerse customers in their narratives. Discover how experiential storytelling transforms passive engagement into active participation.

Imagine experiences as physical spaces where brand narratives come to life. Just as a theater production engages audiences through multisensory experiences, brands can create immersive events and activations that transport customers into their narratives. These experiences serve as stages where stories unfold, allowing customers to actively participate and engage with the brand's narrative in a dynamic way.

Human Touch: Emotional Resonance Through Experiences

Experiences can evoke emotions that touch the core of customers' hearts. Just as memorable experiences leave a lasting impression, brand experiences can create emotional connections that endure. Explore how brands can infuse emotional storytelling into experiential narratives, resonating with customers on a profound level.

Consider the analogy of how unforgettable experiences leave a lasting imprint on individuals, and how brand experiences similarly have the power to create enduring emotional connections. Just as cherished memories from experiences stay with people, brand experiences can create emotional bonds that endure beyond the event itself. Brands can infuse emotional storytelling into their experiential narratives, crafting moments that resonate deeply with customers on a personal and profound level. Explore how brands can design experiential narratives that evoke emotions and touch the core of customers' hearts, fostering connections that go beyond the surface and last over time.

Reimagining Narratives

Narrative Reinvention

Narratives have the power to adapt and transform over time. In this section, we'll explore the concept of narrative reinvention, where brands breathe new life into their stories. Just as stories are retold through various interpretations, brands can reinvent their narratives to captivate new audiences.

Metaphors and Analogies: Narratives as Chameleons

Narratives are chameleons that change colors to fit different contexts. Just as classic tales are reimagined in modern adaptations, brands can reimagine their narratives to reflect changing trends and values. Delve into how brands can keep their narratives fresh and relevant by embracing innovation and reinvention.

Imagine narratives as chameleons that adapt and change colors to seamlessly blend into different contexts. Just as classic tales are reimagined and retold in modern adaptations, brands can also reshape their narratives to align with shifting trends, cultural changes, and evolving values. These adaptive narratives enable brands to remain fresh and relevant, catering to the ever-changing preferences of their audiences.

Contrasting Perspectives: Continuity and Evolution in Narratives

Narrative reinvention balances continuity with evolution. Just as fashion trends revisit past styles with a contemporary twist, brands can revitalize their narratives while retaining core elements. Examine how brands can navigate the tension between familiarity and novelty in narrative reinvention.

Metaphors and Analogies: Narratives as Chameleons

Imagine narratives as chameleons that adapt and change colors to seamlessly blend into different contexts. Just as classic tales are reimagined and retold in modern adaptations, brands can also reshape their narratives to align with shifting trends, cultural changes, and evolving values. These adaptive narratives enable brands to remain fresh and relevant, catering to the ever-changing preferences of their audiences.

Consider how fashion trends often revisit past styles while infusing them with a contemporary twist. Similarly, narrative reinvention requires a delicate balance between continuity and evolution. Brands can breathe new life into their narratives by revitalizing them while still retaining core elements that resonate with their audience. Explore how brands can navigate the tension between familiarity and novelty, reimagining their narratives to incorporate fresh perspectives while preserving the essence of what makes their story unique and engaging.

Navigating Narrative Ethics

Ethical Storytelling

Narratives carry ethical responsibilities, requiring brands to tell stories with integrity. In this section, we'll explore the ethical considerations of narrative crafting. Just as ethical dilemmas arise in literature, brands face ethical dilemmas in storytelling that require careful navigation.

Metaphors and Analogies: Narratives as Moral Tales

Narratives can convey moral lessons that guide audiences' perceptions and choices. Just as fables offer ethical teachings, brand narratives can communicate values and ethical principles. Reflect on how brands can prioritize honesty, authenticity, and transparency in their narratives.

Narratives have the potential to influence society, shaping perceptions and behaviors. Just as impactful literature ignites social movements, brand narratives can drive positive change by addressing societal issues. Explore how brands can use their narratives to inspire, educate, and contribute to broader conversations.

Reflective Closure: The Legacy of Storytelling

As stories endure through generations, so do brand narratives shape a brand's legacy. Reflect on the enduring impact of narratives in the brand landscape. Sum up the section's insights, emphasizing the responsibility brands hold in using narratives to create meaningful connections and inspire ethical action.

Consider how fashion trends often revisit past styles while infusing them with a contemporary twist. Similarly, narrative reinvention requires a delicate balance between continuity and evolution. Brands can breathe new life into their narratives by revitalizing them while still retaining core elements that resonate with their audience. Explore how brands can navigate the tension between familiarity and novelty, reimagining their narratives to incorporate fresh perspectives while preserving the essence of what makes their story unique and engaging.

Amplifying Narratives Through Technology

Tech-Enhanced Narratives

Technology serves as a modern amplifier for narratives, extending their reach and impact. In this section, we'll explore how brands can harness technology to enhance their storytelling. Just as advancements in film enhance cinematic narratives, brands can leverage AR, VR, AI, and other technologies to elevate their narratives to new dimensions.

Metaphors and Analogies: Tech as Narrative Alchemy

Technology transforms narratives into interactive experiences that enchant and captivate. Just as alchemists sought to transmute ordinary elements into gold, brands can use technology to transmute traditional narratives into captivating, multisensory journeys. Dive into how technology augments narratives, adding layers of engagement.

Imagine technology as a modern form of alchemy, capable of transforming traditional narratives into immersive and interactive experiences that captivate and enchant. Just as alchemists sought to transmute base elements into precious materials like gold, brands can use technology to transmute their narratives into captivating, multisensory journeys that resonate deeply with audiences. Technology acts as the catalyst that elevates brand narratives from ordinary to extraordinary, creating experiences that engage and delight.

Reflective Closure: The Fusion of Tradition and Innovation

Just as narratives evolve with time, so do the tools used to tell them. Reflect on how technology reshapes narrative landscapes and amplifies brand stories. Sum up the section's insights, emphasizing the potential of technology to bridge tradition and innovation in narrative crafting.

Reflect on the way narratives have evolved over time, adapting to new tools and mediums, and how technology now reshapes the narrative landscape. Just as narratives evolve, so do the tools used to tell them. Consider how technology bridges the gap between tradition and innovation, allowing brands to infuse their stories with modern engagement techniques while maintaining the essence of their narrative. Sum up the section's insights, emphasizing the profound potential of technology in narrative crafting, and how it allows brands to weave together the timeless power of storytelling with the dynamic capabilities of modern tools.

The Unwritten Narratives

Unseen Narratives

Not all narratives are penned; some unfold silently through actions and experiences. In this section, we'll delve into the concept of unwritten narratives—those communicated through subtleties. Just as subtext speaks volumes in literature, brands can convey powerful messages through their actions and values.

Metaphors and Analogies: Narratives in Gestures

Gestures and actions become the unspoken narratives that audiences interpret. Just as a character's actions reveal their true intentions, brands' actions communicate their values and purpose. Explore how brands can align their actions with their narratives to create authentic and resonant connections.

Imagine that gestures and actions are the unspoken narratives that audiences decode. Just as a character's actions reveal their intentions and personality in a story, brands' actions convey their values, purpose, and identity. These actions become a visual and experiential extension of the brand's narrative, allowing audiences to interpret and connect with the brand on a deeper level.

Contrasting Perspectives: Silence and Resonance

Unwritten narratives rely on silence to resonate with audiences. Just as a pause in music adds weight to the melody, the absence of words in brand actions can speak volumes. Examine how brands can harness the power of silence to convey messages and evoke emotions.

Consider the analogy of how a pause in music adds weight and emotion to the melody. Similarly, in brand actions, the absence of words can often communicate more powerfully than explicit statements. Just as silence in music can evoke emotions, the absence of overt messaging in brand actions can speak volumes, allowing audiences to draw their own interpretations and form emotional connections. Explore how brands can utilize the power of silence and subtlety in their actions to convey messages, evoke emotions, and create a resonance that lingers in the minds and hearts of their audience.

The Legacy of Narratives

Enduring Narratives

Narratives have the potential to outlive their creators and inspire generations to come. In this section, we'll explore the legacy of brand narratives and how they shape a brand's identity over time. Just as classic stories become timeless treasures, brand narratives can become legacies that define a brand's essence.

Metaphors and Analogies: Narratives as Cultural Relics

Narratives evolve into cultural artifacts that capture the spirit of an era. Just as ancient myths hold insights into past civilizations, brand narratives offer glimpses into a brand's journey and values. Reflect on how brands can craft narratives that transcend time, leaving a legacy that resonates for years to come.

Imagine that narratives transform into cultural relics, embodying the essence of a particular era. Just as ancient myths provide insights into past civilizations, brand narratives offer glimpses into a brand's journey, values, and evolution over time. These narratives become valuable artifacts that resonate with audiences and serve as a testament to a brand's identity.

Reflective Closure: The Eternity of Stories

Just as narratives transcend time, so do brand narratives weave a lasting tapestry. Reflect on the enduring impact of narratives on brand perception, loyalty, and legacy. Sum up the section's insights, underscoring the significance of crafting narratives that withstand the tests of time.

Reflect on the way narratives have the power to transcend time, leaving an indelible mark on culture and society. Similarly, brand narratives weave a tapestry that extends beyond the present moment, creating a legacy that resonates for years to come. Consider how brand narratives influence brand perception, foster customer loyalty, and leave a lasting impact on the brand's place in history. Sum up the section's insights, emphasizing the importance of crafting narratives that are not only relevant today but also endure through the ever-changing currents of time.

The Collaborative Narrative

Co-Creative Narratives

Narratives have the power to unite and co-create across diverse perspectives. In this section, we'll explore collaborative narratives—stories that emerge through shared experiences and interactions. Just as a symphony involves multiple musicians, brands can collaborate with customers, employees, and partners to compose narratives that reflect a collective journey.

Metaphors and Analogies: Narratives as Collective Notes

Narratives become collective notes in a symphony of voices. Just as each instrument contributes to the orchestra's harmony, each participant contributes to the narrative's resonance. Delve into how brands can foster co-creative narratives that celebrate diversity and inclusivity.

Imagine that narratives are like individual notes in a symphony, each playing a unique role in the overall harmony. Just as every instrument contributes to the orchestra's symphony, each participant—customers, employees, partners—contributes to the resonance and richness of a brand's narrative. These collective notes come together to create a harmonious narrative symphony.

Human Touch: Embracing Multiplicity

Collaborative narratives emphasize the unity within diversity. Just as a choir blends individual voices into a harmonious melody, collaborative narratives blend various perspectives into a cohesive story. Discover how brands can foster a sense of belonging through narratives that amplify collective voices.

Consider the analogy of a choir where individual voices blend together to create a harmonious melody. Similarly, collaborative narratives emphasize the unity within diversity. Brands can embrace co-creative storytelling, weaving together various perspectives and voices to form a cohesive and inclusive narrative. This approach fosters a sense of belonging, as customers and stakeholders see themselves reflected in the collective story of the brand. Explore how brands can amplify the power of collective voices, celebrating diversity and inclusivity through narratives that resonate with a wide range of individuals.

The Ripple Effect of Narratives

Narratives as Catalysts

Narratives have a ripple effect, sparking conversations and inspiring change. In this section, we'll explore how brand narratives can extend beyond immediate interactions, creating a ripple effect across society. Just as a stone's impact sends ripples through water, narratives can influence perceptions, behaviors, and even social narratives.

Metaphors and Analogies: Narratives as Cultural Waves

Narratives become waves that shape cultural landscapes. Just as cultural movements are propelled by narratives that challenge norms, brand narratives can disrupt and reshape market narratives. Reflect on how narratives can transcend the individual level, impacting collective beliefs and societal perspectives.

Envision narratives as waves that shape the ever-changing landscape of culture. Just as cultural movements are propelled by narratives that challenge existing norms and beliefs, brand narratives have the potential to disrupt and reshape market narratives. These narrative waves create ripples that influence not only individual perceptions but also the broader cultural and societal contexts.

Reflective Closure: Stories That Echo Through Time

Just as ripples echo through water, narratives echo through minds and hearts. Reflect on how brand narratives can drive broader conversations and inspire societal change. Sum up the section's insights, emphasizing the potential of narratives to amplify brand impact beyond immediate interactions.

Reflect on the way ripples in water travel far beyond their point of origin, just as narratives extend their influence beyond immediate interactions. Similarly, brand narratives can drive conversations, spark discussions, and inspire changes in societal perspectives. Consider the lasting impact of narratives that resonate on a cultural level, shaping collective beliefs and influencing societal change. Sum up the section's insights, underscoring the potential of brand narratives to amplify their impact beyond individual engagements, creating a legacy that echoes through time.

The Authenticity of Narratives

Authentic Narrative Craftsmanship

Authenticity is the cornerstone of impactful narratives. Just as a genuine smile resonates more deeply, authentic narratives create emotional bonds that go beyond transactional relationships.

Metaphors and Analogies: Authenticity as Story Foundation

Authenticity is the foundation upon which narratives stand. Just as a solid foundation supports a towering building, authenticity supports narratives that withstand scrutiny. Dive into how brands can infuse their narratives with sincerity, creating stories that resonate with customers' values and beliefs.

Imagine authenticity as the solid foundation upon which narratives are built. Just as a sturdy foundation supports a towering building, authenticity provides the support that allows narratives to stand strong and withstand scrutiny. Without authenticity, narratives would crumble like a structure built on shaky ground. Brands must focus on infusing their stories with sincerity to ensure they resonate with customers' values and beliefs.

Human Touch: Narratives Rooted in Truth

Authentic narratives are rooted in truth and genuine experiences. Just as a trustworthy friend builds deeper connections, brands build trust by sharing honest narratives that align with their actions. Discover how brands can cultivate authenticity by embracing vulnerability and transparency in their storytelling.

Consider the analogy of a trustworthy friend who builds deeper connections through their honesty. Similarly, brands can establish trust with their audience by sharing narratives rooted in truth and genuine experiences. Just as trustworthy friends foster stronger relationships, brands build lasting relationships with customers by embracing vulnerability and transparency in their storytelling. Explore how brands can cultivate authenticity by aligning their narratives with their actions, fostering a sense of trust that strengthens connections and fosters loyalty.

The Infinite Narratives

Narratives Beyond Boundaries

Narratives have limitless potential, transcending geographical and cultural borders. In this section, we'll explore how narratives can resonate universally, making connections across diverse audiences. Just as constellations are visible from different corners of the world, narratives can bridge gaps and create common experiences.

Metaphors and Analogies: Narratives as Global Languages

Narratives become global languages that need no translation. Just as music transcends linguistic barriers, narratives can convey emotions and values universally. Reflect on how brands can craft narratives that appeal to the shared human experiences that bind us together.

Imagine narratives as universal languages that transcend linguistic barriers. Just as music has the power to evoke emotions and convey messages without the need for translation, narratives can communicate emotions, values, and ideas to audiences worldwide. Regardless of cultural and linguistic differences, narratives connect people through shared human experiences.

Reflective Closure: Narratives That Know No Borders

Just as narratives travel beyond borders, so do brand narratives become part of a global conversation. Reflect on how narratives can transcend cultural differences and connect people from various backgrounds. Sum up the section's insights, underscoring the potential of narratives to create bridges of understanding and unity.

Reflect on the way narratives travel freely across borders, just as people do, becoming part of a global conversation. Similarly, brand narratives can transcend cultural and geographical differences, speaking to the shared aspects of the human experience. Consider how narratives have the potential to bridge understanding and create connections between people from diverse backgrounds. Sum up the section's insights, emphasizing the capacity of narratives to break down barriers, foster unity, and create a sense of global togetherness.

The Ethical Narrative

Ethical Storytelling

Ethics are woven into every narrative, shaping perceptions, and fostering trust. In this section, we'll delve into the ethics of storytelling in branding—the responsibility brands have in crafting narratives that uphold honesty and respect. Just as a story's integrity affects its impact, ethical narratives build a foundation of trust with customers.

Metaphors and Analogies: Ethics as Story Pillars

Ethics serve as pillars that support the weight of a narrative's message. Just as architectural integrity ensures a building's stability, ethical storytelling ensures a brand's credibility. Explore how brands can navigate the ethical considerations of narrative creation, enhancing transparency and authenticity.

Envision ethics as the strong pillars that uphold the weight of a narrative's message. Just as architectural integrity ensures a building's stability, ethical storytelling ensures a brand's credibility and reputation. Without ethical considerations, a narrative's structure can crumble, jeopardizing the brand's trustworthiness. Brands must prioritize ethical storytelling to create narratives that stand on solid foundations.

Human Touch: Empathy and Ethical Resonance

Ethical narratives stem from empathy and understanding. Just as empathetic characters engage readers, ethical narratives engage customers by demonstrating respect for their values and concerns.

Discover how brands can embody empathy in their narratives, fostering ethical connections and building lasting relationships.

Consider how empathetic characters in stories deeply engage readers. Similarly, ethical narratives stem from empathy and understanding, addressing customer values and concerns. Brands that embody empathy in their storytelling can create ethical connections with customers, demonstrating a genuine respect for their perspectives. Explore how brands can infuse their narratives with empathy, fostering ethical resonance that builds lasting relationships based on shared values. Ethical storytelling goes beyond mere messaging; it's a commitment to transparency, authenticity, and respect for the audience.

Reflective Closure: Narratives That Stand the Test of Ethics

Just as ethics guide actions, they guide narratives toward enduring impact. Reflect on the ethical considerations that underpin authentic storytelling, and how ethical narratives are more likely to build long-term customer loyalty. Sum up the section's insights, highlighting the importance of narratives that resonate ethically and emotionally.

Immersive Storytelling

Narrative Experiences

Narratives can transcend media, creating immersive experiences that captivate audiences. In this section, we'll explore how brands can leverage immersive storytelling techniques to engage customers in multi-dimensional narratives. Just as a virtual reality experience envelops users, immersive storytelling envelops customers in the world of the brand.

Metaphors and Analogies: Immersion as Story Portal

Immersive storytelling serves as a portal that transports audiences into the narrative world. Just as a doorway leads from one place to another, immersive narratives transport customers from reality into a brand's unique universe. Delve into how brands can create captivating story experiences across various channels and platforms.

Imagine immersive storytelling as a portal that bridges reality and narrative worlds. Just as a doorway leads from one physical space to another, immersive narratives transport customers from their everyday reality into a brand's unique universe. These portals of immersion allow audiences to step into the story, engaging with the brand's narrative on a more profound and interactive level.

Reflective Closure: Crafting Narratives That Immerse

Just as immersion deepens experiences, it deepens brand connections. Reflect on the potential of immersive storytelling to create unforgettable customer interactions. Sum up the section's insights, emphasizing the transformative power of narratives that immerse customers in brand stories.

Consider how immersion deepens the impact of experiences, and similarly, how immersive storytelling deepens brand connections. Reflect on the potential of immersive narratives to create memorable and transformative customer interactions. Sum up the section's insights, emphasizing the significant role of narratives that immerse customers in brand stories, creating connections that are not only engaging but also lasting and impactful.

Storytelling in a Data-Driven World

Crafting Narratives from Data Threads

In this section, we explore how data and storytelling intersect to create narratives that resonate. We'll dive into the art of weaving data threads into compelling stories, whether it's uncovering hidden trends in historical data or using real-time data to craft captivating narratives that captivate audiences. Get ready to see how data storytelling turns numbers into stories that engage, inform, and inspire.

Journalism is undergoing a seismic shift, with data at its core. Investigative reporters are mining datasets to expose corruption, visualizing data to explain complex topics, and using data-driven narratives to shed light on global issues. By blending rigorous analysis with storytelling finesse, these journalists are setting a new standard for impactful reporting.

Visualizing Data: From Charts to Infographics

Charts and graphs are no longer static visuals—they're dynamic tools that bring data to life. In this exploration, we'll uncover the art of data visualization, where designers transform complex data into intuitive and visually appealing representations. From interactive dashboards that let users explore data to infographics that distill information into digestible bites, we'll see how data visualization is a language of its own.

When the COVID-19 pandemic swept the globe, data visualization became a vital tool in understanding its impact. Interactive dashboards tracked cases, deaths, and recoveries in real-time, allowing users to explore trends and patterns. Through color-coded maps, line charts, and dynamic visuals, data visualization conveyed the severity of the situation while empowering individuals with insights to make informed decisions.

Ethical Creativity in a Data-Driven Age

Navigating the Ethical Landscape

With great power comes great responsibility, and data-driven creativity is no exception. In this section, we confront the ethical considerations that arise when working with data. We'll delve into the complexities of data privacy, consent, and bias, exploring how ethical guidelines shape the creative process. From AI-generated content to personal data usage, understanding the ethical implications of data-driven creativity is paramount.

As AI-generated art gains recognition and value, questions about copyright and ownership arise. When algorithms produce art, who owns the rights—the creator or the programmer? Navigating the ethical landscape of AI-generated content requires considering the roles of humans and machines, highlighting the need for clear ethical frameworks in this emerging creative realm.

Narratives: Mental Model

The Narrative Journey Framework

1: Foundation: Authenticity and Ethics

- Foundation Stones: Authenticity and ethics are the solid foundation upon which narratives are built. Just as a sturdy base supports a structure, authenticity and ethics support narratives that withstand scrutiny.

2: Narrative Building Blocks: Elements and Techniques

- Palette of Words: Like a painter's palette, the choice of words creates vivid imagery in narratives.

- Characters as Archetypes: Characters mirror recognizable archetypes that audiences connect with.

- Visual Brushstrokes: Visual elements are brushstrokes that paint the visual narrative.

- Narrative Universes: Brand stories can create immersive worlds, much like alternate realities.

- Ethical Pillars: Ethical considerations uphold narratives, building trust and credibility.

3: Story Arc: Engagement and Transformation

- Arc of Engagement: Narratives follow arcs that keep audiences captivated across touchpoints.

- Brand Journeys as Quests: Brands guide customers through transformative journeys, similar to a hero's quest.

- Narrative Resonance: Impactful endings leave lasting impressions, echoing in the minds of audiences.

4: Audience Engagement: Diversity and Connection

- Collective Notes: Individual voices contribute to a harmonious narrative symphony.

- Global Languages: Narratives transcend linguistic and cultural barriers, connecting people universally.

- Cultural Waves: Narratives shape cultural landscapes, influencing collective beliefs and perspectives.

- Experiences as Narrative Spaces: Immersive experiences become the canvas for brand narratives.

5: Technology and Innovation: Tools for Enhancement

- Tech as Narrative Alchemy: Technology transforms narratives into interactive experiences.

- Narratives in Gestures: Actions and gestures communicate narratives nonverbally.

- Narratives as Cultural Relics: Narratives evolve into cultural artifacts that capture eras.

6: Conclusion: The Power of Narratives

- Legacy and Endurance: Narratives leave lasting legacies, resonating through time.

- Narrative Ecosystem: Brand narratives form a comprehensive ecosystem of stories.

- Symphony of Stories: Various narratives harmonize to create a rich brand experience.

7: Key Principles:

- Authenticity and Ethics: Authenticity is the heart, and ethics are the backbone of narratives.

- Diversity and Connection: Narratives connect diverse voices and cultures.

- Engagement and Transformation: Narratives guide audiences through transformative journeys.

- Innovation and Enhancement: Technology elevates narratives, enhancing engagement.

- Impact and Legacy: Narratives leave a legacy, resonating across time.

Outcome: The Narrative Journey Framework emphasizes the power of narratives to connect, engage, and resonate. By crafting authentic, diverse, and immersive stories, brands create lasting connections, shape cultural landscapes, and leave an indelible legacy that echoes through time.

Crafting Resonant Legacies

As we bring our exploration of this segment to a close, we find ourselves standing at the crossroads of imagination and reality, where stories become the very lifeblood of branding's transformative journey. Just as a captivating story lingers in the mind, the narratives we've delved into resonate deeply within the heart of every brand, shaping the very essence of its identity.

From the foundational pillars of authenticity and ethics to the symphonic harmony of narratives that orchestrate brand experiences, we've traversed the profound power of storytelling in modern branding. These narratives extend beyond the digital realm, beyond market landscapes, and even beyond cultural borders, leaving an indelible mark that echoes across time.

As we reflect on the journey that led us here, let's draw strength from the compelling statistics that affirm the influence of storytelling in the realm of branding:

Storytelling Statistics:

1. According to a survey by Edelman, 81% of consumers cited brand trust as a major factor in their purchasing decisions, underscoring the importance of narratives grounded in authenticity.

2. A study by Kantar Millward Brown revealed that ads with strong storytelling outperform those without by 21% in terms of long-term brand engagement.

3. HubSpot's research demonstrates that companies consistently utilizing storytelling in their marketing strategies experience

revenue growth 2.5 times faster compared to those neglecting narrative elements.

4. A survey by Adobe uncovered that 58% of consumers are likely to remember content featuring a compelling narrative, compared to just 20% for content devoid of storytelling.

5. Google's insights highlight that YouTube ads enriched with storytelling elements, such as emotional resonance and relatable characters, enjoy 3 times higher ad recall and purchase intent.

This part has been a journey—a passage from brand-as-a-platform to the narrative-driven resonance that propels modern branding. Along this path, we've seen the strategic deployment of narratives not only as communicative tools but as conduits of emotional connection, yielding loyalty and enduring relationships.

Guided by the "Narratives," you now possess the means to harness narratives as transformative agents within the modern branding landscape. The key lies in crafting narratives that bridge gaps, transcend boundaries, and resonate with diverse cultures— narratives that lay the foundation for trust, engagement, and resonance with your audience.

As you stand poised at this juncture, envision a road ahead shaped by your ability to create narratives that transcend the limits of time, cultural nuances, and ever-shifting trends. The insights shared and statistics presented in this part serve as guiding lights, illuminating a path toward narratives that leave an indelible legacy within the hearts and minds of your customers.

But let us not forget the wisdom of Ashwath Damodaran, whose perspective highlights that narratives are not merely soft constructs but powerful drivers that impact financial and branding realms alike. Just as narratives shape investor perceptions, they shape customer perceptions, loyalty, and a brand's ultimate bottom line. The power of narratives extends beyond numbers, infusing identity with meaning, purpose, and resonance.

In weaving the insights of Ashwath Damodaran into our narrative journey, we uncover the intersection of financial value and emotional impact. Just as narratives influence a company's market value, they also influence a brand's emotional value in the hearts of its customers.

As we bid adieu to the "Narratives" let these insights and reflections linger as beacons, guiding you forward as you craft narratives that captivate, resonate, and leave an enduring mark. Through the lens of storytelling, you've seen how brands can be both narrators and listeners, engaging in conversations that forge authentic connections.

The journey from brand-as-a-platform to narrative-driven resonance has been a voyage of evolution and enlightenment. As you navigate the road ahead, remember that the narratives you craft are not just stories—they are integral to your brand's identity, connecting with audiences across cultures and forging a legacy that transcends time.

Thank you for joining this exploration of "Narratives." As you persist in crafting stories that inspire, resonate, and leave a lasting impression, may your tales reverberate in the hearts and minds of your audience, continually molding the story of your brand's evolution.

Reflections

Brand Story

Key Points	Description
The Power of Storytelling	In today's world of fragmented media and short attention spans, mastering the art of storytelling is essential for brands to connect deeply with their customers.
Starting with "Why"	Effective storytelling begins by articulating an organization's purpose and passion—answering the "why"—to engage consumers and convey the core values that drive the brand.
Examples of Compelling "Why"	Illustrative examples include Intel, Apple, and Google, who used taglines to articulate their corporate strategy, making people genuinely care about their brand's promise. Nescafe Philippines' "Red Mug Sessions" successfully tapped into community spirit through the love of music.
Empowering and Engaging	Beyond just narration, brands should empower their audience to actively participate in a two-way dialogue. Real-time marketing, exemplified by Oreo's Super Bowl tweet, enables audiences to co-create brand narratives.
Purpose and Relevance	Effective stories have a clear message or purpose that creates relevance and meaningful connections with the audience. Brands like Zappos and SingTel co-create their purpose with consumers, resulting in a more resonant brand promise.

Key Points	Description
SingTel's Real-time Success	SingTel's bold venture into real-time marketing, where they engaged followers to describe scenarios for 4G usage, not only boosted engagement but also drove traffic to their 4G website. This exemplifies the potential of co-creating relevant brand stories.
Stories over Data	The most successful brand storytellers are akin to meaning-makers. They craft emotionally resonant stories that inspire and motivate their audience, emphasizing that stories, not mere data, are what truly connect people.

Your Strategy Needs a Story

Key Points	Description
Strategy and Storytelling	While business strategy is typically rooted in facts and analysis, storytelling, often associated with fiction, can complement strategy. It is not the opposite of strategy but a powerful tool to bridge strategy and action. Stories have the capacity to engage, motivate, and drive action, making them crucial in strategy communication and implementation.
The WCS Elephant Conservation	The Wildlife Conservation Society's (WCS) strategy to save elephants provides an example of an effective strategy story. The WCS employed storytelling to rally support and action against elephant poaching, trafficking, and demand for ivory. It showcased the power of narrative in driving significant conservation efforts through coalition-building and legislative changes.

Key Points	Description
Strategy: Beyond Rationality	While a well-structured strategy is vital, it alone may not inspire action or be fully understood. A study revealed that only a small percentage of managers could name their firm's strategic priorities. Strategy stories bridge the gap between strategy documents and practical action by offering a narrative that engages and motivates people.
The Power of Narrative	Stories are narratives designed to engage and impact an audience. Humans comprehend the world through stories, and stories have evolved to transmit information effectively. Stories, unlike dry facts and statistics, can move people to action. They provide a framework for understanding complex situations and are adaptable to changing circumstances, making them ideal for today's fast-paced, competitive world.
Storytelling in Marketing and Strategy	The business world acknowledges the power of storytelling in marketing, as exemplified by campaigns like Nike's "Just Do It." Storytelling can also be harnessed in business strategy to create something new and valuable. Strategies are stories that begin in the present and resolve in the undetermined future.
Collaborative Strategy Building	Traditional strategy has been an elite activity, but openness and collaboration are emerging trends in strategy development. Collaborative tools like Zoom, Slack, and AirBoard allow companies to involve employees close to customers, competitors, and implementation in the strategy creation process. An open approach can result in more effective, comprehensible, and owned strategies.

Key Points	Description
Constructing a Strategy Story	Building a strategy story involves establishing a factual context, leveraging questions to invite exploration, writing a narrative that encompasses the past, present, and future, testing the story with internal and external audiences, and ensuring that the story is concise, engaging, and motivating. The story should be relatable and understandable in a short time, focusing on central issues. Consistent repetition and discussion are essential for understanding and retention.
The Value of Strategy Stories	Strategy stories connect context and intent by making complex strategies understandable and relatable. They transform facts and information into shared mental models of how a business operates and where it's headed. Constructing strategy stories as shared, adaptable mental models can improve implementation and accelerate a company's learning rate, offering a competitive advantage in today's rapidly changing business environment.

PART-5

DESIGNING CUSTOMERS, NOT PRODUCTS

SHAPING DESIRES AND DESTINIES

Shaping Desires and Destinies

Introduction: Shaping the Customer-Centric Paradigm

In an era of swiftly changing customer preferences, thriving brands recognize that sustained growth doesn't just come from creating products, but from designing experiences that deeply connect with their customers. Welcome to this segment, where we set off on an enlightening journey to discover the art of designing with the customer as the focal point of every decision.

From the initial spark of an idea to the final touchpoint of interaction, this part delves into the principles and strategies that guide brands towards customer-centric design. Just as the preceding parts—Brand as a Platform, Revenue Subscribed, and Algorithmic First—paved the way for evolving branding paradigms, we now delve into the realm where design takes center stage, placing customers at the forefront of the process.

In a rapidly evolving world characterized by complexity, uncertainty, and an incessant stream of challenges, the ability to innovate and find creative solutions has never been more crucial. Enter design thinking—a dynamic and human-centered approach that empowers individuals and organizations to tackle problems, generate ideas, and shape the future in innovative ways. Beyond the realm of aesthetics, design thinking is a mindset, a methodology, and a philosophy that transcends disciplines, industries, and boundaries.

Imagine a world where problems are opportunities waiting to be seized, where empathy fuels innovation, and where collaboration and experimentation are celebrated. This is the essence of design thinking—a journey that empowers us to understand people's needs deeply, challenge assumptions, and redefine problems to uncover fresh insights. It's a journey that turns uncertainty into opportunity and fosters a culture of continuous learning and improvement.

Here, we will delve into the multifaceted world of design thinking, exploring its principles, methodologies, and applications across various domains. We will journey through the stages of empathetic problem framing, ideation, prototyping, testing, and implementation, uncovering how each step contributes to the creation of user-centric, innovative solutions. We will also navigate the key mindsets and traits that define successful design thinkers—curiosity, open-mindedness, resilience, and a willingness to learn from failure.

But design thinking isn't limited to designers alone; it's a toolkit that anyone can wield to drive meaningful change. Entrepreneurs, engineers, educators, healthcare professionals, policymakers, and individuals from all walks of life can harness its power to revolutionize their fields and create positive impact. Design thinking is the bridge that connects human needs with technological advancements, blending the analytical and the intuitive to yield breakthroughs that are both functional and emotionally resonant. As we embark on this exploration of design thinking, we invite you to embrace curiosity, adopt a beginner's mindset, and challenge the status quo. Together, we will unravel the mysteries of empathy-driven problem solving, discover the beauty of iteration, and witness the transformation that occurs when we put the needs of people at the heart of innovation. Whether you're new to the concept or a seasoned practitioner, this guide will equip you with the knowledge, tools, and inspiration to embark on your own design thinking journey and make a lasting impact on the world around you.

Empathy-Driven Design

The Role of Empathy in Design

Empathy is the brushstroke that paints masterpieces of design. Just as a portrait artist captures the essence of their subject's soul, brands must step into the lives of their customers to truly understand their needs, desires, and pain points. In this section, we embark on an exploration of how empathetic design breathes life into customer experiences, forging genuine connections that resonate.

Human-Centered Insights: Designing with Empathy

Empathetic design is a journey through the landscapes of customer experiences. It's about understanding their aspirations, struggles, and aspirations, then crafting solutions that meet them where they are. Think of Airbnb's "Experiences" feature, where hosts offer personalized activities that cater to travelers' interests and passions. By deeply comprehending the diverse needs of their customers, Airbnb empowers hosts to create experiences that transcend traditional accommodations, fostering connections that go beyond the transactional.

Customer Journeys: Mapping Emotions

A customer journey is a symphony of emotions, with crescendos of excitement and moments of introspection. Just as a conductor orchestrates harmonies, brands can map customer journeys to craft experiences that evoke emotions at each touchpoint. Take Apple's retail stores, where every step—entering, exploring, interacting—is designed to evoke feelings of excitement, curiosity, and discovery. Through mapping emotional touchpoints, Apple crafts an experience that resonates deeply, leaving a lasting imprint on customers' hearts and minds.

Behavioral Insights in Design

Unveiling the Power of Behavior

Understanding customer behaviors is akin to deciphering a complex puzzle. Just as a detective piece together clues to solve a case, brands decode behaviors to design interactions that seamlessly fit into customers' lives. This section unveils the art of leveraging behavioral insights to craft experiences that intuitively align with customers' actions and intentions.

Behavioral Design: Guiding Choices

Behavioral design is the compass guiding customers toward desired actions. Like a trail of breadcrumbs leading through a forest, brands can design pathways that nudge customers toward beneficial decisions. Consider Netflix's binge-watching model, which artfully capitalizes on the human desire for completion. By auto playing the next episode of a series, Netflix fosters engagement, enhancing the user experience and driving customer satisfaction.

Nudging and Decision Architecture: Shaping Outcomes

Decisions are often influenced by the context in which they're made. Just as an architect designs spaces to evoke specific feelings, brands can shape decision-making contexts to drive desired outcomes. Think of Starbucks' mobile app, nudging users to join the Starbucks Rewards program and earn points with each purchase. By architecting the decision-making process, Starbucks increases customer engagement, aligning choices with the brand's vision and customers' aspirations.

Co-Creation and Collaboration

Co-Creation as a Bridge

In a world where collaboration is the heartbeat of innovation, co-creation bridges the gap between brands and customers. Much like a symphony is co-created by an orchestra's harmonious collaboration, brands can co-create with customers to craft experiences that resonate deeply. This section illuminates the transformative power of involving customers in the design process.

Customer Co-Creation: Building Together

Co-creation is a canvas where customers become artists. Just as an architect collaborates with clients to design their dream homes, brands can invite customers to contribute to the design of products and services. LEGO's Ideas platform is a prime example—by allowing customers to submit designs for potential new LEGO sets, the brand taps into creativity, fostering a sense of ownership among fans, and co-creating products that resonate authentically.

Shared Experiences: From Participation to Advocacy

Shared experiences forge bonds stronger than steel. Just as friends sharing an adventure create enduring memories, co-created experiences between brands and customers build camaraderie. Consider Nike's "Nike by You" program, where customers can customize their sneakers. This co-creation process empowers individual expression, forming an emotional bond with the brand. Customers who co-create their own Nike sneakers transition from participants to brand advocates, sharing their unique designs and experiences.

Emotional Resonance through Design

Designing for Emotional Impact

At the heart of human experiences lie emotions, waiting to be stirred. Just as a painter uses colors to evoke feelings, brands can design interactions that resonate emotionally. This section unveils the intricacies of designing for emotional resonance, where every touchpoint becomes a canvas for crafting profound connections.

Emotionally Intelligent Design: Crafting Feelings

Emotionally intelligent design is a symphony of feelings. Like a poet meticulously selecting words, brands use design elements to evoke desired emotions. Imagine Coca-Cola's holiday campaigns, using festive packaging and heartwarming stories to tap into customers' emotions, creating joy and connection during the holiday season. This strategy forges a strong emotional bond between the brand and its customers, transcending mere consumption.

Aesthetic Value: The Beauty of Connection

Aesthetic design isn't skin-deep—it's the language of connection. Like a photographer capturing a fleeting moment's essence, brands design touchpoints that capture their identity's very essence. Consider Tesla's electric vehicles, not just efficient machines but aesthetic statements. The sleek, minimalist design and attention to detail reflect the brand's values, resonating with customers who seek both elegance and functionality.

Inclusivity in Design

Designing for Diverse Experiences

In a world that celebrates diversity, designing for inclusivity is not just a choice—it's a responsibility. Just as a welcoming host ensures everyone feels at home, brands can create experiences that resonate with diverse audiences. This section delves into the art of inclusivity in design, where every touchpoint embraces the richness of human differences.

Designing for Accessibility: Beyond Barriers

Inclusivity starts with accessibility! Just as an architect designs ramps for wheelchair users, brands can craft experiences that break down digital and physical barriers. Microsoft's adaptive controller for gaming is a testament to this approach, making gaming more inclusive for people with limited mobility. By designing for accessibility, brands create spaces where everyone can engage, fostering connections and empowerment.

Cultural Sensitivity: Navigating Diversity

Culture weaves a tapestry of experiences, each thread adding vibrancy and depth. Just as a traveler learns local customs, brands must be culturally sensitive in their design. Airbnb's "Open Homes" initiative exemplifies this by connecting travelers with hosts from diverse backgrounds, promoting cross-cultural understanding. Through culturally sensitive design, brands can celebrate differences and create spaces where every individual feels seen and respected.

Evolving Identities: Gender-Inclusive Design

Identities are as fluid as water, transcending traditional definitions. Brands can embrace gender-inclusive design to reflect and honor the spectrum of identities. Non-binary fashion lines, such as Phluid Project, offer clothing that defies conventional gender norms, creating spaces where self-expression is limitless. By designing with gender inclusivity in mind, brands foster a sense of belonging for all individuals, promoting authenticity and connection.

Sustainability in Design

Designing for a Better Planet

The world's future depends on sustainable choices. Just as a gardener tends to a flourishing ecosystem, brands can design experiences that promote environmental well-being. This section explores the intersection of design and sustainability, where each touchpoint becomes an opportunity to nurture our planet.

Ecological Consciousness: Beyond Consumption

Sustainability is more than a buzzword—it's a commitment to the planet. Brands like Patagonia exemplify ecological consciousness through design by crafting durable, long-lasting products. This approach challenges the culture of disposable consumerism, promoting a more thoughtful relationship with possessions. Through ecological consciousness, brands inspire customers to be stewards of the Earth, forging a bond rooted in shared values.

Circular Design: Redefining Endings

In a linear world of "take, make, dispose," circular design offers a new narrative. Just as an alchemist transforms base materials into gold, brands can design products and experiences that embrace circularity. H&M's "Looop" machine, which upcycles old clothing into new garments, showcases circular design's potential. By extending the lifespan of products, brands contribute to a sustainable future while fostering a sense of responsibility among customers.

Ethical Sourcing: Stories of Origin

Every product carries a story, from inception to creation. Brands can design with ethical sourcing in mind, ensuring that every thread, ingredient, or material is sourced responsibly. Companies like TOMS, which pioneered the "One for One" movement, prioritize ethical sourcing while giving back to communities in need. Ethical sourcing design not only creates quality products but also weaves narratives of positive impact, connecting customers to the broader global community.

Designing for Digital Experiences

Navigating the Digital Landscape

In a digitally interconnected world, brands transcend physical boundaries through digital experiences. Just as a digital artist molds virtual sculptures, brands can design digital touchpoints that captivate and engage. This section navigates the realm of digital design, where pixels and code converge to create memorable interactions.

User-Centered Interfaces: Intuitive Pathways

Digital design is a dance of pixels and pathways. Just as a choreographer orchestrates movements, brands design interfaces that guide users seamlessly. Google's search interface exemplifies user-centered design by providing a clean, intuitive layout. By crafting interfaces that anticipate users' needs, brands create digital experiences that resonate, fostering connection and engagement.

Multi-Platform Consistency: A Unified Journey

In a multi-screen world, consistency is the glue that binds experiences together. Just as an author maintains a consistent narrative voice, brands can design across platforms to ensure a unified customer journey. Coca-Cola's branding maintains consistent elements across digital touchpoints, reinforcing its identity regardless of where customers interact. By designing for multi-platform consistency, brands create a cohesive narrative, enhancing recognition and connection.

Responsive Experiences: Adapting to Context

Digital experiences are like chameleons, adapting to their environment. Just as a chameleon changes color to blend in, brands can design responsive experiences that adapt to various devices and contexts. Amazon's responsive design allows customers to seamlessly transition between devices while maintaining a coherent experience. Through responsive design, brands ensure that their interactions remain engaging and accessible, regardless of how customers engage.

Crafting Ethical Design

The Moral Compass of Design

Design carries an inherent responsibility—to create experiences that are not only captivating but also ethically sound. Just as a moral compass guides explorers, brands can navigate ethical design principles to ensure their touchpoints align with values and respect for users. This section delves into the ethics of design, where every decision reflects a commitment to integrity and authenticity.

Transparency in Design: Honoring Trust

Transparency is the cornerstone of ethical design. Just as a glass house invites openness, brands can design experiences that prioritize transparency in data collection and usage. Apple's privacy-focused approach exemplifies this, giving users control over their data and setting a new standard for industry ethics. Through transparent design, brands build trust and foster a sense of security, creating connections rooted in honesty.

Inclusive Representation: Amplifying Voices

Design is a platform for amplifying voices that have long been silenced. Just as a megaphone magnifies a speaker's words, brands can design touchpoints that feature diverse representation. Adobe's "Stock" platform offers inclusive stock photos that reflect a wide range of ethnicities, abilities, and backgrounds. Inclusive representation design not only reflects the world's diversity but also empowers marginalized communities, fostering connections built on mutual respect.

Ethical Algorithms: Navigating Complexity

In an algorithm-driven world, ethical considerations extend beyond design aesthetics. Just as a navigator charts a course through uncharted waters, brands can design algorithms that prioritize fairness and avoid bias. Spotify's algorithmic playlists balance personalization with diversity, ensuring that users are exposed to a range of music styles. Ethical algorithm design acknowledges the power algorithms hold and strives to create experiences that empower rather than discriminate, fostering connections grounded in equity.

Privacy-Centric Design

Respecting Digital Boundaries

In an era of data-driven interactions, respecting users' privacy is paramount. Just as a courteous host respects guests' personal space, brands can design experiences that prioritize user privacy and data security. This section delves into privacy-centric design, where every touchpoint upholds users' digital boundaries and builds trust.

Data Minimization: Collecting with Purpose

Less is more when it comes to data collection. Just as a minimalist artist captures essence with few strokes, brands can design experiences that collect only the necessary data for seamless interactions. Signal, a privacy-focused messaging app, exemplifies data minimization by storing minimal user information. By designing with data minimization in mind, brands create experiences that safeguard users' privacy while still offering valuable interactions.

User Consent: Empowering Choice

Consent is the cornerstone of ethical data usage. Just as a consent form informs participants before an experiment, brands can design experiences that empower users to make informed choices about their data. GDPR-compliant websites, for example, offer clear consent prompts for data collection. By prioritizing user consent, brands foster a sense of control and respect, creating connections built on transparency.

Anonymous Engagement: Privacy without Sacrifice

Privacy and personalization can coexist. Just as a masked ball allows attendees to interact without revealing identities, brands can design experiences that enable anonymous engagement while still offering value. Reddit, a platform built around user-generated content, allows users to engage without revealing personal information. By designing for anonymous engagement, brands extend connections to those who value privacy and encourage authentic interactions.

Gamification in Design

Turning Engagement into Play

Incorporating elements of play into design can transform engagement into an immersive experience. Just as a game captivates players with challenges and rewards, brands can design touchpoints that utilize gamification to enhance interactions. This section explores the art of gamification in design, where engagement is no longer a transaction but a playful journey.

Points, Badges, and Rewards: Navigating Challenges

Gamification often revolves around rewards and achievements. Just as a scout earns badges for mastering skills, brands can design experiences that reward users for engaging with their products or services. Duolingo, a language-learning app, uses this approach by awarding points and badges for completing lessons. By integrating points, badges, and rewards, brands turn engagement into a game, fostering a sense of accomplishment and motivation.

Narrative Structure: Crafting Stories of Interaction

Stories engage and immerse us in worlds beyond our own. Just as a novelist weaves plots and characters, brands can design experiences with a narrative structure that guides users through their interactions. Nike's "Nike Training Club" app adopts a narrative structure, leading users through personalized fitness journeys. By employing narrative elements, brands create journeys that resonate emotionally, deepening connections and enhancing engagement.

Competition and Collaboration: Fostering Community

Games often foster both competition and collaboration among players. Just as a team collaborates in a sport, brands can design experiences that encourage users to compete or collaborate for shared goals. Fitbit, a fitness tracking device, introduces challenges that allow users to compete with friends and colleagues. By fostering competition and collaboration, brands create communities where users feel connected through shared experiences and goals.

Multisensory Experiences

Sensory Symphony in Design

Human experiences are multisensory, engaging sight, sound, touch, taste, and smell. Just as a symphony conductor orchestrates a harmonious blend of instruments, brands can design experiences that engage multiple senses for a more immersive connection. This section explores the art of crafting multisensory experiences that transcend the visual, creating profound connections through sensory stimuli.

Sensory Branding: Crafting Unique Signatures

Brands can be recognized by more than just their logos; they can be identified by their sounds, scents, and tactile sensations. Just as a musician's melody becomes their signature, brands can design multisensory elements that distinguish them. Intel's sonic logo, for example, is a distinct audio identity that reinforces the brand's presence. By integrating sensory branding, brands create holistic experiences that leave lasting impressions.

Haptic Feedback: Touching Digital Realms

In a digital age, touch is not limited to the physical world. Just as a blind person reads Braille, brands can design interactions that incorporate haptic feedback, allowing users to feel responses in a digital environment. Video game controllers with vibration feedback, like those used in console gaming, provide an immersive experience by translating digital actions into tactile sensations. By integrating haptic feedback, brands bridge the gap between physical and digital interactions, enriching engagement.

Synesthetic Design: Blurring Boundaries

Synesthesia is a neurological phenomenon where one sensory experience triggers another. Just as a visual artist might perceive colors while listening to music, brands can design experiences that elicit synesthetic responses, engaging multiple senses simultaneously. Absolut Vodka's "Absolut Colors" campaign, which associated cocktail flavors with colors, is an example of synesthetic design. By intertwining sensory experiences, brands create layered connections that stimulate emotions and memories.

Adaptive and Inclusive Design

Design for All

Design should not exclude anyone; it should be inclusive and accessible to all individuals, regardless of their abilities. Just as a ramp enables wheelchair users to access a building, brands can design experiences that cater to diverse needs. This section delves into adaptive and inclusive design, where every touchpoint is created with empathy and consideration for all users.

Universal Design Principles: Bridging Gaps

Universal design principles prioritize accessibility from the outset. Just as a universally designed door lever accommodates both hands, brands can design experiences that are inherently accessible to a wide range of users. Microsoft's inclusive design toolkit, for example, ensures that products are usable by people with varying abilities. By implementing universal design, brands bridge gaps and create experiences that welcome everyone.

Assistive Technologies: Enabling Accessibility

Technology has the power to enable accessibility for individuals with disabilities. Just as a guide dog assists a visually impaired person, brands can design experiences that work seamlessly with assistive technologies, such as screen readers or voice commands. Apple's VoiceOver feature, which provides spoken descriptions of on-screen elements, enhances accessibility for blind users. By embracing assistive technologies, brands ensure that their experiences are usable and enjoyable for all users.

Inclusive Visual and Interaction Design: Beyond Aesthetics

Inclusivity goes beyond technical considerations; it extends to the very essence of design. Just as diverse representation enriches a story, brands can design visuals and interactions that reflect the diversity of their audience. Google's Emoji Kitchen, which allows users to create unique emojis by combining existing ones, encourages diverse self-expression. By crafting inclusive design elements, brands foster a sense of belonging and make all users feel valued.

Ethical and Sustainable Design

Designing for a Better World

Design has the capacity to shape not only experiences but also the world around us. Just as an architect designs sustainable buildings that minimize environmental impact, brands can design experiences that prioritize ethical and sustainable practices. This section explores the role of design in driving positive change and creating a more equitable and environmentally conscious world.

Ethical Design Principles: Prioritizing Values

Ethical design considers the broader societal impact of products and experiences. Just as an ethical code guides professionals' conduct, brands can design with principles that prioritize user well-being and societal benefit. Mozilla, for instance, promotes ethical design through its "Privacy Not Included" campaign, which evaluates the privacy and security aspects of smart devices. By integrating ethical considerations, brands build trust and contribute to a safer digital landscape.

Sustainable Innovation: Designing for Longevity

Sustainable design focuses on minimizing waste and extending the lifecycle of products and experiences. Just as a circular economy aims to eliminate waste, brands can design experiences that are built to last and can be easily repurposed or upgraded. Patagonia's "Worn Wear" program, which encourages customers to buy and sell used clothing, embodies sustainable innovation. By designing for longevity, brands reduce their environmental footprint and promote responsible consumption.

Design for Social Impact: Catalyzing Change

Design can drive positive social change by addressing pressing societal issues. Just as a campaign raises awareness about a cause, brands can design experiences that amplify social impact. TOMS Shoes' "One for One" initiative, where a pair of shoes is donated for every pair sold, exemplifies design for social impact. By incorporating social responsibility into design, brands contribute to meaningful change and create experiences that resonate beyond commerce.

Future-Focused Design

Embracing the Unknown

The future of design is an open canvas, waiting to be painted with innovation and imagination. Just as an explorer venture into uncharted territory, brands can embrace the unknown and push the boundaries of design. This section delves into the frontiers of design's evolution, exploring emerging technologies and trends that will shape the experiences of tomorrow.

Design and Artificial Intelligence: A Synergistic Future

Artificial intelligence (AI) is revolutionizing design by augmenting creativity and efficiency. Just as a collaborator enhances an artist's work, AI can assist designers in generating ideas and predicting user preferences. Adobe's "Sensei" AI platform, which enhances design workflows, exemplifies the synergy between design and AI. By embracing AI, brands can unlock new levels of innovation and create experiences that are both personalized and efficient.

Virtual and Augmented Reality: Designing Immersive Realities

Virtual reality (VR) and augmented reality (AR) offer new dimensions of immersive experiences. Just as a storyteller creates fictional worlds, brands can design virtual environments that engage users in unprecedented ways. Pokémon GO, an AR game that overlays digital creatures onto the real world, showcases the potential of AR. By designing for VR and AR, brands can create experiences that blur the lines between physical and digital realms.

Designing for the Metaverse: A New Reality

The metaverse is an interconnected virtual space where digital and physical experiences converge. Just as a metropolis brings together diverse communities, brands can design experiences that transcend individual platforms and exist within the metaverse. Facebook's rebranding to "Meta" and its vision for a metaverse future illustrate this evolution. By designing for the metaverse, brands can create seamless and interconnected experiences that redefine human interaction.

Designing for Inclusivity and Diversity

Empowering Every Voice

Design is a powerful tool that can either reinforce existing biases or break down barriers. Just as a diverse ensemble of musicians creates harmonious melodies, brands can design experiences that embrace inclusivity and diversity. This section delves into the importance of designing for all voices, ensuring that every user feels represented and empowered.

Inclusive Design Principles: Accessibility for All

Inclusive design ensures that products and experiences are accessible to individuals of all abilities. Just as a ramp allows people with mobility challenges to access a building, brands can design digital experiences that cater to a wide range of users. Microsoft's Inclusive Design toolkit, which provides guidelines for creating accessible products, demonstrates the commitment to inclusivity. By designing with accessibility in mind, brands create experiences that resonate with diverse audiences.

Cultural Sensitivity in Design: Global Perspectives

Design transcends borders, but it must also respect and reflect different cultural contexts. Just as a translator bridges language gaps, brands can design experiences that resonate with various cultural nuances. Airbnb's efforts to ensure cultural sensitivity in its platform, such as offering diverse representation in its photography, exemplify this approach. By embracing cultural diversity, brands foster connections and create experiences that resonate on a global scale.

Gender-Inclusive Design: Breaking Stereotypes

Design has the power to challenge gender norms and stereotypes. Just as a gender-neutral bathroom accommodates all identities, brands can design experiences that are inclusive of diverse gender expressions. The "All Types All Swipes" campaign by Tinder, which introduces more inclusive gender options for users, illustrates the importance of gender-inclusive design. By dismantling assumptions, brands create spaces where users can authentically express themselves.

The Impact of Design Leadership

Nurturing a Culture of Design

Design leadership goes beyond individual projects; it shapes organizational culture. Just as a conductor leads an orchestra to create symphonies, design leaders guide teams to craft experiences that align with the brand's vision. This section explores the role of design leadership in fostering innovation, collaboration, and a commitment to excellence.

Design-Driven Innovation: Leading with Creativity

Design leaders inspire innovation by fostering a culture that embraces experimentation and creative thinking. Just as a trailblazer charts a new course, design leaders empower teams to explore uncharted territories. Apple's design philosophy, influenced by Steve Jobs, exemplifies the impact of design-driven innovation. By championing creativity, design leaders pave the way for breakthrough experiences that captivate audiences.

Collaborative Design Culture: Uniting Diverse Expertise

Design is a collaborative endeavor that thrives on diverse perspectives. Just as a mosaic pieces together various colors and shapes, design leaders foster environments where cross-functional teams contribute their expertise. IDEO's interdisciplinary approach to design thinking showcases the power of collaboration. By cultivating a culture of inclusivity and shared ownership, design leaders drive holistic and user-centered solutions.

Design Ethics and Responsibility: Guiding Principles

Design leaders have a responsibility to uphold ethical standards and consider the broader impact of their work. Just as a moral compass guides ethical decisions, design leaders prioritize user well-being and societal benefit. Tim Cook's emphasis on user privacy and Apple's commitment to data protection highlight design ethics. By leading with integrity, design leaders shape experiences that not only delight users but also contribute positively to society.

The Future of Design: Emerging Trends and Possibilities

Shaping Tomorrow's Experiences

The design landscape is constantly evolving, driven by technological advancements, shifting user expectations, and societal changes. Just as a futurist envisions possibilities, this section peers into the crystal ball to explore the emerging trends that will shape the future of design. From augmented reality to sustainable design, the future promises new horizons for designers to explore.

Augmented Reality and Immersive Experiences: Beyond the Screen

Design is no longer confined to two-dimensional screens—it's expanding into the realm of augmented reality (AR) and immersive experiences. Just as a magician blurs the line between reality and illusion, designers are crafting digital worlds that seamlessly integrate with our physical environment. The rise of AR applications like Pokémon GO and IKEA's AR furniture shopping exemplifies the potential of immersive experiences. By merging the digital and physical, designers create novel ways for users to interact and engage.

Sustainable and Eco-Friendly Design: Designing for Tomorrow's World

The urgency of environmental challenges is reshaping design's role in sustainability. Just as a conservationist protects ecosystems, designers are embracing eco-friendly practices that minimize environmental impact. The Cradle-to-Cradle design approach, championed by brands like Patagonia, emphasizes sustainable materials and circular design principles. By prioritizing sustainability, designers contribute to a more sustainable and regenerative future.

Neuro design and Emotional AI: Designing for the Mind

Advances in neuroscience and artificial intelligence are opening new avenues for understanding user behavior and emotions. Just as a psychologist deciphers thought patterns, designers are incorporating emotional AI to create experiences that resonate on a deeper level. The use of emotional AI in chatbots and virtual assistants, like Woebot, illustrates the potential of neurodesign. By tailoring experiences to users' emotional states, designers create more empathetic and engaging interactions.

Designing for Social Impact

Design as a Catalyst for Change

Design is a powerful tool for addressing societal challenges and driving positive change. Just as an activist rally for justice, designers can use their skills to tackle issues ranging from inequality to public health. This section explores how design can be harnessed as a catalyst for social impact, sparking conversations and driving transformation.

Design for Social Equality: Bridging Gaps

Design can bridge the gaps that divide society, promoting inclusivity and social equality. Just as an architect designs accessible buildings, designers can create products and experiences that empower marginalized communities. The "Accessible Icon Project," which redesigns the traditional wheelchair symbol, exemplifies design's potential for social change. By challenging norms and advocating for inclusivity, designers become agents of social progress.

Public Health and Behavior Change: Designing for Well-Being

Design can influence behavior and promote healthier lifestyles. Just as a public health campaign encourages vaccination, designers can craft interventions that nudge users towards positive choices. The "Nudge Unit" in the UK government demonstrates how behavioral insights can drive change. By using design to encourage healthy habits and preventative measures, designers contribute to improved public well-being.

Design Activism: Amplifying Voices

Designers have a unique platform for amplifying important messages and advocating for justice. Just as an artist's mural conveys a powerful message, designers can use their visual language to spark conversations and raise awareness. The "Design for Good" movement, championed by organizations like AIGA, exemplifies how design can be a force for positive change. By using their skills to address social issues, designers become advocates for a better world.

Ethical Considerations in Design

The Moral Imperative of Design

Designers wield immense influence over user experiences and perceptions. Just as an ethical philosopher contemplates right and wrong, designers must grapple with the ethical implications of their creations. This section delves into the complex landscape of ethical considerations in design, exploring the responsibilities designers have in shaping interactions that are respectful, transparent, and fair.

Privacy and Data Ethics: Protecting User Rights

In an era of data-driven experiences, designers must prioritize user privacy and data ethics. Just as a lawyer upholds legal rights, designers must safeguard user information and ensure transparent data practices. The "Privacy by Design" framework, championed by organizations like the International Association of Privacy Professionals, emphasizes incorporating privacy considerations from the outset of design. By respecting user autonomy and protecting their data, designers foster trust and accountability.

Inclusive Design and Accessibility: Designing for All

Designers have a moral obligation to create inclusive experiences that cater to diverse user needs. Just as a civil rights advocate fights against discrimination, designers must challenge barriers to accessibility. The Web Content Accessibility Guidelines (WCAG) provide a blueprint for inclusive web design, ensuring that digital experiences are usable by everyone, including those with disabilities. By considering diverse perspectives and needs, designers contribute to a more equitable and inclusive digital world.

Ethical AI and Algorithm Design: Avoiding Bias and Harm

As AI becomes integral to design, designers must grapple with ethical considerations surrounding algorithmic decision-making. Just as an ethicist scrutinizes the consequences of actions, designers must ensure AI systems are fair, unbiased, and responsible. The "AI Ethics Guidelines" developed by organizations like IEEE highlight the importance of transparency, accountability, and avoiding bias in AI design. By embedding ethical considerations into AI systems, designers mitigate potential harm and ensure that technology serves humanity's best interests.

Designing for the Unknown: Embracing Uncertainty

Navigating the Uncharted Waters

The design landscape is in constant flux, with new challenges and opportunities emerging unpredictably. Just as an explorer embarks on uncharted journeys, designers must be adaptable and open to change. This section delves into the mindset required to navigate uncertainty and the strategies designers can employ to thrive in ever-evolving design ecosystems.

Design Thinking and Iterative Prototyping: Embracing the Process

In a rapidly changing world, designers must embrace iterative and agile approaches to problem-solving. Just as a scientist refines hypotheses through experimentation, designers must iterate on concepts to achieve optimal outcomes. Design thinking methodologies, such as the Stanford d. school's five-stage process, emphasize empathy, ideation, prototyping, and testing. By continually refining designs based on user feedback, designers adapt to evolving needs and deliver solutions that resonate.

Resilience and Adaptability: Thriving Amidst Change

Designers must cultivate resilience and adaptability in the face of uncertainty. Just as a resilient ecosystem withstands disturbances, designers must anticipate change and pivot when necessary. The concept of "antifragility," introduced by Nassim Nicholas Taleb, suggests that systems can become stronger in response to shocks. By adopting a mindset that embraces change as an opportunity for growth, designers can navigate uncertain terrain with confidence.

Design Ethics and Sustainability

The Nexus of Design and Sustainability

In an era of environmental consciousness, designers hold the power to drive sustainable change. Just as an environmentalist advocate for the planet's health, designers must integrate sustainability into their creations. This section delves into the intersection of design ethics and sustainability, exploring how designers can prioritize eco-friendly practices and contribute to a more sustainable future.

Circular Design: Redefining Consumption

Designers play a pivotal role in shifting from a linear "take-make-dispose" model to a circular one. Just as an ecologist studies ecosystems, designers must consider the lifecycle of products and materials. The concept of circular design emphasizes design for durability, repairability, and recyclability. By designing products that can be easily repaired, repurposed, or recycled, designers reduce waste and promote a more sustainable consumption culture.

Environmental Impact Assessment: Designing Responsibly

Designers must assess the environmental impact of their creations, just as a conservationist evaluates ecosystem health. Tools like Life Cycle Assessment (LCA) allow designers to quantify the environmental footprint of products and make informed decisions. By considering factors like carbon emissions, resource consumption, and pollution, designers can make choices that minimize negative impacts and contribute to a healthier planet.

Biophilic Design: Nurturing Human-Nature Connections

Biophilic design is a response to humanity's disconnect from the natural world. Just as a biologist studies interactions between organisms, designers explore ways to integrate nature into the built environment. Incorporating elements like natural light, greenery, and natural materials enhances well-being and fosters a sense of connection with nature. By creating spaces that evoke the tranquility and vitality of natural environments, designers promote sustainable lifestyles and attitudes.

The Future of Design: Emerging Frontiers

Designing for Tomorrow's Horizons

Design is on a perpetual journey of evolution, venturing into uncharted territories. Just as a futurist envisions new possibilities, designers must anticipate emerging trends and technologies. This section explores the exciting frontiers that lie ahead for design, shaping the course of industries, societies, and human experiences.

Immersive Experiences and Extended Reality: Designing Alternate Realities

The convergence of virtual reality (VR), augmented reality (AR), and mixed reality (MR) presents new opportunities for designers. Just as a storyteller weaves narratives, designers create immersive experiences that blur the lines between physical and digital realms. As extended reality becomes more integrated into everyday life, designers must master the art of crafting compelling and meaningful experiences that engage users in novel ways.

Biomimicry and Nature-Inspired Design: Learning from Nature

Nature has perfected designs over billions of years, making it a valuable source of inspiration for designers. Just as a biomimicry enthusiast studies organism for innovation, designers can draw from nature's solutions to complex problems. By emulating nature's patterns, structures, and processes, designers can develop sustainable, efficient, and adaptable solutions across various industries.

Ethical Considerations in AI and Automation: Human-Centric Design

As AI and automation continue to shape industries, designers must address ethical dilemmas surrounding technology's impact on society. Just as an AI ethicist contemplates the consequences of automation, designers must prioritize human well-being and values. The principles of value-sensitive design and ethical AI underscore the importance of designing technology that respects human autonomy, fairness, and transparency. By upholding ethical standards, designers ensure that AI enriches human lives without compromising fundamental rights.

Design Customers: Mental Model

Imagine a spiral staircase, ascending from a foundation of knowledge and gradually unfurling toward the pinnacle of innovation. This is the Transformational Design Spiral, a dynamic mental model that encapsulates the iterative process of design evolution. Each step of the spiral represents a distinct stage in the journey, where principles, strategies, and creativity intertwine to shape the future of design.

1. **Foundation of Understanding:** At the base of the spiral lies the Foundation of Understanding. Here, designers immerse themselves in the essence of their audience, their culture, and their context. Just as an archaeologist uncovers artifacts to decipher history, designers unearth insights to comprehend the intricate tapestry of human needs, emotions, and behaviors.

2. **Empathy-Driven Exploration:** Moving upward, the spiral advances into Empathy-Driven Exploration. Designers step into the shoes of their audience, cultivating deep empathy. Like a navigator mapping uncharted terrain, they chart emotional landscapes, understand pain points, and illuminate aspirations. This empathetic voyage informs every design decision, as designers strive to create experiences that resonate profoundly.

3. **Behavioral Insights Ascendancy:** Continuing the ascent, the spiral enters the realm of Behavioral Insights Ascendancy. Here, designers harness the power of human behavior, much like a conductor orchestrates a symphony. By decoding behavioral cues, they anticipate actions and

reactions, skillfully guiding users toward desired outcomes. This strategic choreography transforms design into a harmonious dance of intentions and actions.

4. **Collaborative Innovation Nexus:** Climbing higher, the spiral reaches the Collaborative Innovation Nexus. Designers embrace collaboration as a compass, just as explorers' partner with fellow adventurers. Through co-creation, they transcend individual limits, infusing diverse perspectives and talents. This nexus becomes a melting pot of ideas, where collective imagination births solutions that surpass solitary vision.

5. **Emotionally Resonant Apex:** The spiral's apex unveils the Emotionally Resonant Apex—an ethereal realm where design transcends functionality and becomes an art form. Like a composer evoking emotions through music, designers craft experiences that stir the soul. This realm is adorned with emotionally intelligent design elements—colors, textures, and narratives—evoking feelings that linger in the heart and memory.

6. **Aesthetic Ethos Alchemy:** Descending gracefully, the spiral enters the Aesthetic Ethos Alchemy—a place where form and meaning fuse seamlessly. Designers channel their inner alchemists, transforming visual aesthetics into vessels of purpose. Just as a painter selects hues to convey emotions, designers craft touchpoints that mirror the very essence of brands, forging connections beyond the surface.

7. **Ethical Design Nexus:** Further down the spiral lies the Ethical Design Nexus—a juncture of conscience and creation. Here, designers grapple with the ethical implications of their work, akin to philosophers pondering the morality of actions. As custodians of experiences, they weigh the impact on society, culture, and the environment, ensuring that design resonates ethically with the greater good.

8. **Innovation's Horizon:** Completing the spiral, designers arrive at Innovation's Horizon—a vantage point that gazes upon the limitless potential of the future. Like astronomers peering into the cosmos, designers envision new frontiers. It is here that the spiral intersects with innovation, where design becomes a catalyst for transformation, pushing boundaries and shaping a world yet to be realized.

Experiential Design Mastery: Exercises for Transformative Innovation

In this comprehensive collection, we embark on a journey to explore the dynamic realm of experiential design—a realm where innovation isn't just a concept, but a tangible and transformative process. Whether you're a seasoned designer, an aspiring entrepreneur, or simply someone curious about crafting exceptional experiences, this collection of exercises offers you the tools and insights to master the art of creating experiences that leave a lasting impact.

As we navigate through this experiential design journey, we'll delve into the principles, strategies, and techniques that underpin transformative innovation. This isn't just about aesthetics or functionality; it's about crafting experiences that resonate deeply with people, fostering connections that go beyond transactions. We'll explore the spectrum of design elements, from empathy-driven insights to behavioral nuances, from co-creation to emotional resonance. Each exercise is carefully crafted to challenge your perspective, stimulate your creativity, and ultimately elevate your ability to design experiences that matter.

The exercises within this collection are designed to be immersive and interactive. They encourage you to step into the shoes of your users, embrace uncertainty, and think beyond the surface. As you engage with these exercises, you'll be guided through thought-provoking scenarios, real-world examples, and hands-on activities that encourage you to put theory into practice. Along the way, you'll sharpen your design skills, cultivate your empathetic understanding, and refine your ability to create transformative experiences that resonate with people on a profound level.

The journey ahead is an exploration of the transformative power of design—a power that transcends the boundaries of products and services to shape the very way people interact, connect, and live their lives. So, whether you're seeking to enhance your professional skills, reimagine your business strategies, or simply nurture your curiosity, prepare to immerse yourself in the world of experiential design mastery. Let's embark on this transformative journey together and discover the endless possibilities that arise when innovation meets human-centered design.

The Transformational Design Spiral is a journey of perpetual growth, an ever-expanding vista of creativity, empathy, and evolution. With each turn, designers ascend and descend through these stages, continuously refining their craft. Just as the spiral has no end, the quest for transformative design remains an enduring pursuit—infusing humanity with inspiration, purpose, and connection.

1. **Empathy Immersion Expedition:** To cultivate empathy by experiencing the world through the eyes of others.

   Instructions: Choose a target audience segment, such as a specific age group, profession, or cultural background. Spend a day immersing yourself in their world—consume their media, visit their spaces, and engage with their activities. Document your observations and reflections on their needs, emotions, and behaviors. Use this newfound empathy to brainstorm design ideas that cater to their unique perspectives.

2. **Behavioral Analysis Adventure:** To uncover behavioral insights that can guide design decisions.

   Instructions: Select a product or service and identify a key user action you want to encourage. Observe potential users interacting with the product/service, either in person or through user recordings. Analyze their behaviors, emotions, and decision-making processes. Based on your findings, design small nudges or modifications that encourage the desired behavior. Test these interventions and iterate based on the outcomes.

3. **Collaborative Ideation Workshop:** To harness diverse perspectives and co-create innovative design solutions.

   Instructions: Gather a diverse group of individuals from various disciplines and backgrounds. Present them with a design challenge or problem statement. Encourage each participant to contribute ideas, building on one another's thoughts. Use techniques like brainstorming, mind mapping, and rapid prototyping to generate a range of design concepts. By collaborating and weaving together these diverse insights, craft a holistic solution.

4. **Emotion-Centric Storyboarding:** To design experiences that evoke specific emotions at each touchpoint.

   Instructions: Choose a brand or product you want to enhance with emotional resonance. Create a storyboard that maps out the customer journey, illustrating each touchpoint along the way. For each touchpoint, identify the desired emotion you want to evoke. Craft visuals, narratives, and design elements that align with that emotion. This exercise helps you align the design elements with the intended emotional impact.

5. **Ethical Design Dilemma Deliberation:** To consider the ethical implications of design decisions.

   Instructions: Present participants with a series of design scenarios that involve ethical considerations, such as privacy concerns, environmental impact, or cultural sensitivity. In groups or individually, discuss and debate the potential ethical dilemmas posed by each scenario. Consider the broader societal implications and weigh the trade-offs involved in different design choices.

6. **Aesthetic Interpretation Experiment:** To understand the interplay between aesthetics and brand identity.

   Instructions: Choose a well-known brand and analyze its visual identity, including logo, color palette, typography, and design elements. Create a mood board or collage that captures the essence of the brand's aesthetics. Now, reinterpret the brand's identity using a different visual style—for example, if the brand is minimalist, reimagine it with maximalist elements. Reflect on how these changes affect the brand's perception and resonance.

7. **Future-Focused Design Visioning:** To envision innovative design solutions for the future.

   Instructions: Research emerging technologies, social trends, and cultural shifts. Identify a trend or technology that is likely to influence design in the future. Imagine how this trend might impact user behaviors and needs. Design a product, service, or experience that leverages this trend to create value. Focus on how the design aligns with the Transformational Design Spiral's principles to shape the future.

Pioneering the Uncharted, Crafting Tomorrow

In the ever-evolving tapestry of human creativity, the role of design shines as a guiding star, illuminating the path toward a future filled with possibilities. As we embark on this visionary journey into the future of design, we embrace the spirit of pioneers, driven to shape the unknown and craft a tomorrow that exceeds today's imagination.

Throughout the parts and sections of this exploration, we have delved into the multifaceted realms of design—unveiling its power to shape perceptions, transform experiences, and foster connections that transcend time and space. Just as a captain navigates uncharted waters, designers are at the helm, steering industries, cultures, and human experiences toward horizons yet to be discovered.

From the foundational principles of branding that establish identities and foster loyalty, to the intricate dance of empathy and behavioral insights that design the very fabric of interactions, each facet of design weaves a tapestry of influence. Co-creation sparks collaboration, emotional resonance forges connections, and ethical considerations light the way to a responsible future. With each brushstroke of emotionally intelligent design, we create symphonies of feelings that echo through generations.

As we conclude this journey, let us remember that the canvas of design is not limited to pixels and paper—it extends to every facet of existence, from products to spaces, from technology to culture. With courage, innovation, and an unwavering commitment to creating positive change, designers will continue to pioneer the uncharted and breathe life into the dreams of tomorrow.

In a world ever in flux, where the only constant is change itself, design stands as the cornerstone of our ability to shape the future. It is a beacon that guides us toward a more empathetic, sustainable, and harmonious world. So, let us continue to be the architects of experience, the poets of emotion, and the visionaries of innovation. For in the grand tapestry of existence, it is design that weaves the threads of human imagination into the fabric of reality, crafting tomorrow from the uncharted realms of today.

Reflections

Challenge	Design Thinking Approach	Transformed Outcome	Trapped Value Unleashed
Enterprises grapple with the confines of their expertise and past experiences.	Shift focus to 'Design Customers' rather than just products.	Achieve a profound and empathetic understanding of their intended customers.	Unleashes untapped user insights and unmet needs, leading to innovative solutions.
Enterprises, drowning in a sea of complex qualitative data, seek a lifeline.	Serves as a guiding light, distilling the chaos into elegant patterns, and steering enterprises towards...	Discovering exhilarating insights and uncharted horizons.	Unleashes hidden opportunities and potential in the data, sparking innovative ideas.
Enterprises, grappling with the cacophony of divergent team voices, seek harmony.	Acts as the conductor, translating insights into actionable design notes, and guiding innovation teams towards...	Attaining harmonious resonance with users, akin to a symphony in perfect harmony.	Unleashes the power of teamwork, combining diverse perspectives to create user-centric solutions.

Challenge	Design Thinking Approach	Transformed Outcome	Trapped Value Unleashed
Enterprises, lost in a wilderness of fragmented ideas, yearn for a trail to follow.	Becomes the navigator, cutting through the underbrush with focused inquiry, and directing team members towards...	An expedition through a curated jungle of ingenious solutions, each a treasure waiting to be unearthed.	Unleashes a multitude of innovative concepts, providing a rich landscape of possibilities.
Enterprises, ensnared by their preconceived notions, crave clarity.	Becomes the torchbearer, illuminating the path with explicit prerequisites for success, and propelling teams towards...	A crystal-clear understanding of pivotal assumptions, like a clear night sky revealing the stars.	Unleashes the power of clear thinking, removing obstacles to innovation.
Enterprises, seeking user feedback amidst a fog of uncertainty, need a beacon.	Becomes the lighthouse, casting its light on rudimentary prototypes, offering enterprises an opportunity to...	Gain precise feedback and a genuine understanding of the solution's intrinsic value, akin to a safe harbor in the storm.	Unleashes valuable insights from user feedback, guiding product refinement.
Enterprises, trembling at the precipice of change, yearn for a steady hand.	Becomes the guide, leading them through practical experiments with staff and users, helping them in...	Cultivating unwavering confidence and commitment to the innovative product or strategy, like a trusted sherpa guiding a mountain ascent.	Unleashes a culture of resilience and adaptability, enabling innovation in turbulent times.

Challenge	Design Thinking Approach	Transformed Outcome	Trapped Value Unleashed
Enterprises, struggling to adapt in a rapidly shifting landscape, seek a compass.	Becomes the compass, encouraging continuous adaptation and iteration, guiding enterprises to...	Navigate the ever-changing terrain with agility and foresight, like a seasoned sailor steering through unpredictable waters.	Unleashes the potential to stay ahead of market changes and seize opportunities.
Enterprises face the elusive trapped value gap, yearning for liberation.	Acts as the liberator, unveiling hidden user desires, reconciling user, and business objectives, and igniting a cultural revolution, thus...	Unlocking untapped treasures, mitigating risks, promoting interdisciplinary harmony, weaving compelling stories, embracing inclusivity, nurturing long-term value, and wielding design as a competitive weapon.	Unleashes a wealth of value previously locked away, transforming the innovation landscape.

Conclusion: Crafting Your Singular Path in the Realm of Brand Building

As our odyssey through the domains of "Finding Your B.R.A.N.D." gracefully nears its zenith, we arrive at a pivotal crossroads. Much like a medieval fortress fortified by its protective moat, this literary voyage has guided you in erecting an impervious bastion of competitive distinction within the intricate tapestry of brand building.

Our expedition has transcended mere wanderlust; it has metamorphosed into an epiphany. We've traversed beyond the shallows of exploration, unearthing the secret to businesses transcending the relentless torrents of competition. We've delved into the enigmatic depths of differentiation, uncovered the hidden jewels of customer-centricity, and dissected the time-worn blueprints of triumphant enterprises.

Equipped with this treasury of revelations, you stand on the precipice of shaping your brand's formidable B.R.A.N.D. Yet, bear in mind, a B.R.A.N.D. is not a solitary confinement; it's a beacon, a sanctuary beckoning customers in search of the extraordinary. It's the creation of an identity that radiates so uniquely that mimicry becomes a futile endeavor.

Reflect on the sagacity shared by entrepreneurs and visionaries whose tales have illuminated our path. Their narratives have underscored the valor of resilience and the alchemy of innovation. A thriving B.R.A.N.D. is not a static bulwark; it's a fluid entity that rides the currents of change while retaining its essential essence.

In the same manner that grand castles exhibit unique architectural styles, your brand boasts its own defining attributes that serve as the very foundations of your B.R.A.N.D. Whether it's the narrative that threads through your brand's fabric, the excellence radiating from your offerings, the bonds you nurture, or the transformative experiences you bestow, your B.R.A.N.D. awaits fortification and celebration.

Ultimately, the pursuit of your B.R.A.N.D. isn't a formulaic exercise in branding mechanics; it's a testament to your ardor, your steadfast commitment, and your tireless quest for excellence. It signifies that your brand stands as a tribute to innovation, a haven of value, and a guardian of customer fidelity.

As you march onward, embrace the path that is unmistakably yours. Assemble your B.R.A.N.D. with surgical precision, safeguard it with an unwavering gaze, and watch it gleam as the emblem of your brand-building expedition. Amidst the ever-shifting panorama of brands, let your B.R.A.N.D. stand as the embodiment of your unyielding devotion to your craft, your clientele, and your vision. And remember, your B.R.A.N.D. is not solely a bulwark – it's the bedrock upon which your brand will flourish, engraving an indelible legacy across your industry and beyond.

Acknowledgments: A Symphony of Collaborative Melodies

In the narrative tapestry of "B.R.A.N.D.," we have interwoven a symphony, each chapter a distinct movement, varying in rhythm and emotion, animated by an extraordinary ensemble of souls. Everyone has infused a unique note into this communal opus, enriching it with their singular melodies.

A Standing Ovation for My First Maestro: My Father, A. Venkatraman

Picture a mentor who not only ushered me into the realm of business but also embodied the essence of perpetual learning - that was my late father, A. Venkatraman. Dad, your relentless curiosity, and your sagacious counsel during our dawn promenades have been the cornerstone of my odyssey. Your wisdom echoes throughout this volume, a tribute to the virtues you bestowed with such fervor.

The Resilient Beacon: My Mother Vijayalakshmi Venkatraman

To my mother, a lighthouse of hope in the most turbulent seas. Mom, your resilience, especially during our clan's challenging relocation, and your unwavering optimism have been my beacon. You imparted that with hope and perseverance, every hurdle can be surmounted. Your indomitable spirit illuminates every leaf of this tome.

The Pillars of Insight

Immeasurable gratitude to the trailblazing entrepreneurs, sage business leaders, and avant-garde thinkers who imparted their narratives. Your insights, like the dialogues about daring ventures, have been pivotal in sculpting this book's chronicle.

The Orchestra of Unwavering Support

To my family, friends, and allies, you have been the rhythmic heartbeat of my journey, pulsating with support and inspiration. My siblings – Indira, Kannan, and Vanitha – and their families have crafted an irreplaceable tapestry of companionship and empathy around me. This includes my siblings-in-law, Dr. Balaji, Dr. Krishnan Suresh, and Anu Kannan, along with our uncles, aunts, and their respective children, whose steadfast presence and support have been a constant through the years. Their soothing words in moments of uncertainty have been the harmonious undertones that have gently buoyed me through this voyage.

To Ranjani, my consort in life, your unshakable faith during the nascent stages of the book's concept has been the cornerstone of its inception. And to Rithvik and Rithanyaa, my beloved children, your affection and patience have been the sanctuary of this artistic endeavor. In you, I have found a bastion of strength and tranquility, the serene core in the whirlwind of creative pursuit.

A Tribute to Endless Vitality: Dr. K.A. Jagannathan

To my uncle, Dr. K.A. Jagannathan, on the cusp of 90 yet embodying an explorer's spirit. Your enthusiasm for existence, be it your latest marine adventure or your voracious reading, is a profound inspiration, a reminder that passion and curiosity are ageless.

The Pillars of our Family: My In-Laws

To my in-laws, your steadfast support, especially during our nascent parenting years, has been a godsend. Your dedication and affection have been crucial threads in the last 26+ years of our union.

Deep Appreciation for Mentorship

I am profoundly grateful for the mentorship and guidance provided by Sivakumar Venkataramany, Professor of International Business at Ashland University, during my formative years. His support, along with that of his mother, who was a strong advocate for me, has been invaluable. My gratitude for their help is immense and enduring.

The Artisans Behind the Scenes

Foremost, profound gratitude to Miki Trikha and Vijaya Desikan from the Rezilyens Operations squad. Over a decade of your allegiance, commitment, and priceless contributions, particularly imaginative solutions to our formidable challenges, have been fundamental in the triumph of our endeavors.

To the editors, designers, researchers, and publishers – your exceptional skills have propelled "B.R.A.N.D." to its highest point of achievement. Each of you, particularly Lasyashree, Venkat Raman, Vikram Krishnaraya, Rajesh Rengarajan, Abishek Radhakrishnan, Seshadri Rengarajan, Rithanyaa Venkat, Santhanam Balaji, Vanitha Suresh, Kannan Venkatraman, Kimberly Quiambao, and the staff at Notion Press, have significantly contributed to enhancing this project. Your unique talents and diligent research have beautifully showcased our collective effort.

Special appreciation is extended to Madhu Ranganathan, CFO of OpenText, for her perceptive book review and valuable feedback. Her extensive financial acumen has added significant depth and professionalism to the narrative.

Deep gratitude to Vijay Sridharan and his wife Revathi, Gautham Padmanabhan in Operations, and the HR team comprising Ramya and Sangeetha, for their exceptional support in managing our dual residency in India and the USA. Their dedication and skill in navigating international work arrangements have been pivotal in ensuring a smooth transition and continuous global engagement.

A heartfelt acknowledgment to Dhanish, whose commitment and coaching expertise have been transformative for my son Rithvik, who has autism. Dhanish's mentorship has not only fostered Rithvik's growth as a promising yoga instructor and bachelor's degree student but has also made him an inspiring figure for many.

Within the business sector, I wish to particularly highlight a group of people who have played the roles of friends, ex-colleagues, clients, and key influencers throughout my journey. Notably, Krish Mani, Donald Morris, Jeff Wiggin, Tony Dudek, Kirthy Chennaian, Duane Kunze, Grant Ecker, and Jeff Winter, among others, deserve mention, albeit in no order. I'm aware there are many more I haven't named, but it was important for me to acknowledge at least a few.

Their fellowship, insights, and challenges have been a constant source of inspiration and encouragement in my journey to write this book. Their collective wisdom and experiences have been invaluable in shaping both my career and the perspectives shared in "B.R.A.N.D."

Special recognition to Anand Palanisamy and Kimberly Quiambao for their outstanding roles in project management and chief of staff responsibilities. Their exceptional organizational skills, strategic planning, and unwavering support in pivotal projects have been crucial in allowing me the time to bring these book's concepts and strategies to fruition.

And to the several others who have crossed paths with me, your stories, challenges, and victories have been a wellspring of inspiration, urging me to capture the essence of our shared experiences in this book.

The Heart of the Symphony: My Readers

To you, the readers, your engagement, and application of these principles are the lifeblood of this book. I eagerly anticipate your insights and stories of growth, making this a shared voyage of discovery.

The Unseen Muses

And to the myriad of authors, thinkers, and creators whose works have inspired my imagination and informed my thoughts, your influence flows silently yet powerfully through my writing.

In Finale

This acknowledgment is a tribute to every individual who has been part of this symphony, directly or indirectly. Your contributions, support, and inspiration have composed this melody of learning and success.

With deepest appreciation,

Ranghan Venkatraman

Sign Off: The Final Note in Our Ode to Winning

As the curtain slowly falls on our shared journey through "B.R.A.N.D.," it's time to savor the final note of this extraordinary ode to winning. We ventured together not just as readers and writer, but as partners in the pursuit of victory, each page a step in the dance of differentiation and triumph.

The Crescendo of Our Collective Pursuit

Our voyage began with an audacious notion – to transform the concept of winning in the relentless arena of modern business. We traversed the nuances of creating brands that don't just exist but thrive, resonate, and lead. From the artful symphonies of brand differentiation to the strategic harmonies of innovative market approaches, and the emotional resonance of genuine connections, we've explored the multifaceted dimensions of winning.

The Resonance We Carry Forward

As you step away from the closing lines of this book, let the echoes of its melodies linger in your approach to winning. The strategies, insights, and narratives woven through these parts are not mere words; they are the instruments of your victory orchestra, awaiting your command to create an enduring legacy.

An Unending Symphony of Success

The conclusion of "B.R.A.N.D." is not an end, but a grand interlude. The true performance commences as you apply these lessons to your personal and professional quests. The symphony of your success is an ever-unfolding narrative, evolving with every strategic move, every innovative idea, every meaningful connection you forge.

The Conductor's Baton in Your Hand

As you turn the final page, hold onto the sense of empowerment it brings. You are the conductor of your winning saga. Armed with the baton of knowledge and insight from this book, you possess the power to orchestrate a narrative of success that resonates with your audience, distinguishes you in the market, and withstands the test of time.

Encore: A Continuous March Towards Mastery

Remember, the quest for winning is a perpetual performance, filled with evolving challenges, opportunities, and arenas. Let the wisdom of "B.R.A.N.D." be your guide, your inspiration, as you continue to navigate the intricate dance of success with creativity, strategic acumen, and an unwavering commitment to excellence.

A Parting Note, But Not a Farewell

As we part ways at this juncture, let this book be a beacon on your journey towards winning. May your endeavors be a symphony that others look to for inspiration, a testament to your skill, creativity, and mastery in the art of winning.

Thank you for allowing me to be a part of your journey to triumph. Here's to the majestic music you will compose in the vast concert hall of business and life. Until our paths cross again in the pursuit of excellence, continue to wield your conductor's baton with bravery, vision, and an indomitable spirit to win.

Welcome to B.R.A.N.D. – where every aspiration is a movement, every achievement a melody, and every triumph a timeless symphony.

With heartfelt gratitude and best wishes for your unending symphony of success,

Ranghan Venkatraman

Afterword

While delving into "B.R.A.N.D.", an unforeseen melody echoed through its pages – a harmony weaving the mystique of musical language with the meticulous realm of technology. The author's ingenuity in employing the musical lexicon as a lens to demystify intricate technical conundrums is nothing short of brilliant.

Admittedly, before opening this book, my grasp of Artificial Intelligence and its profound impact on modern management was limited. However, as I journeyed deeper into its chapters, the undying symphony of music began to seamlessly merge with AI's cutting-edge algorithms, presenting a perspective hitherto unexplored.

Drawing inspiration from the triadic elegance of a three-movement musical piece, the narrative introduces an insightful metaphor for unraveling complex problems. Hegel's dialectical triad – thesis, antithesis, and synthesis – is mirrored in this musical arrangement. One can't help but speculate if the philosopher's seminal thought structure was, perhaps, influenced by the traditions of Western classical music.

As you, dear reader, set forth on this harmonious expedition, be prepared to unveil the synergies between the worlds of music and technology – two domains often seen in contrast, yet masterfully juxtaposed here to enrich our collective comprehension.

With anticipation and admiration,

Dr. K.A. Jagannathan, Ph.D.

About the Author

Ranghan Venkatraman's remarkable career showcases a unique combination of breadth and depth across multiple industries. His roles as CEO and CTO in a variety of award-winning companies, including Rezilyens, Pinochle.AI, and Kyureeus, along with his experience at prestigious organizations like Deloitte and major corporations such as Intel, The Home Depot, and Grainger, underline his exceptional leadership capabilities. Furthermore, his involvement in international forums such as The World Economic Forum (Davos) underscores his significant influence in the realms of business and technology.

Venkatraman's prowess as a keynote speaker is notable, with his ability to simplify and convey complex ideas in a manner that is both engaging and inspiring, impacting professionals in numerous fields. His role as a Forbes contributor further showcases his thought leadership, providing valuable perspectives on current and evolving issues in business and technology.

A key focus area for Venkatraman is Algorithmic Business Physics, where he is dedicated to unraveling technological and business potential using first principles thinking. His passion lies at the crossroads of business, technology, and entrepreneurship, where he propels innovation through state-of-the-art technology platforms.

Additionally, Venkatraman is preparing for the launch of his next book, 'Seamless Minds.' This book promises to delve into the fascinating interplay of generative AI and human intelligence, a realm where Venkatraman has shown substantial expertise. Anticipated to offer unique insights into the synergy between advanced AI technologies and human creativity, this publication is set to further cement his position as a foremost thinker in the field.

References

Part 1

1. Smith, A. B. (2020). The Art of Branding. HarperCollins.

2. Johnson, M. (2018). Branding with a Twist: A Guide to Adding Humor to Your Brand. Creative Publishing.

3. Moon, Y. (2010). Different: Escaping the Competitive Herd. Crown Business.

4. Aaker, D. A. (2014). Aaker on Branding: 20 Principles That Drive Success. Morgan James Publishing.

5. Keller, K. L. (2013). Strategic Brand Management: Building, Measuring, and Managing Brand Equity. Pearson Education.

6. Grant, A. (2018). Originals: How Non-Conformists Move the World. Penguin Books.

7. Kotler, P., Kartajaya, H., & Setiawan, I. (2016). Marketing 4.0: Moving from Traditional to Digital. Wiley.

8. Pine II, B. J., & Gilmore, J. H. (1999). The Experience Economy: Work Is Theater & Every Business a Stage. Harvard Business Press.

9. Brown, T. (2009). Change by Design: How Design Thinking Transforms Organizations and Inspires Innovation. HarperBusiness.

10. Prahalad, C. K., & Ramaswamy, V. (2004). The Future of Competition: Co-Creating Unique Value with Customers. Harvard Business Press.

11. HBR: Transitioning Your Company from Product to Platform by Nathan Furr

Part 2

1. Tzempelikos, N., Gounaris, S., & Chatzipanagiotou, K. (2019). Subscription-based pricing strategies: Customer value, business model and innovation. Journal of Business Research, 94, 137-146.

2. Anderson, C. K., & Narus, J. A. (2003). Business market management: Understanding, creating, and delivering value. Pearson Education.

3. Anderson, R. E., & Srinivasan, S. S. (2003). E-satisfaction and e-loyalty: A contingency framework. Psychology & Marketing, 20(2), 123-138.

4. Fader, P., Hardie, B., & Lee, K. L. (2005). RFM and CLV: Using iso-value curves for customer base analysis. Journal of Marketing Research, 42(4), 415-430.

5. Amazon Prime. (n.d.). About Amazon Prime. Retrieved from https://www.amazon.com/amazonprime

6. Dollar Shave Club. (n.d.). Why We're Better. Retrieved from https://www.dollarshaveclub.com/how-it-works

7. Adobe Creative Cloud. (n.d.). Features. Retrieved from https://www.adobe.com/creativecloud/features.html

8. Birchbox. (n.d.). Why Birchbox. Retrieved from https://www.birchbox.com/about/birchbox-uk

9. Apple Music. (n.d.). Apple Music: What's Inside. Retrieved from https://www.apple.com/apple-music/features/

10. Ipsy. (n.d.). How it Works. Retrieved from https://www.ipsy.com/about/ipsy-subscription/

11. Stitch Fix. (n.d.). How It Works. Retrieved from https://www.stitchfix.com/how-it-works

12. Dollar Shave Club. (n.d.). How It Works. Retrieved from https://www.dollarshaveclub.com/how-it-works

13. Netflix. (n.d.). Pricing. Retrieved from https://help.netflix.com/en/node/24926

14. Spotify. (n.d.). Premium: Listen without ads on Spotify. Retrieved from https://www.spotify.com/premium/

15. HelloFresh. (n.d.). How It Works. Retrieved from https://www.hellofresh.com/about/how-it-works/

16. HBR Ascend. (2020). Can Subscription Services Predict Consumer Behavior? Retrieved from https://hbrascend.org/topics/can-subscription-services-predict-consumer-behavior/

Part 3

1. HBR Algorithms Can Make Your Organization Self-Tuning by Martin Reeves

2. Russell, S., & Norvig, P. (2016). Artificial Intelligence: A Modern Approach. Pearson Education.

3. Davenport, T. H., & Ronanki, R. (2018). Artificial Intelligence for the Real World. Harvard Business Review.

4. Bughin, J., Hazan, E., Ramaswamy, S., Chui, M., Allas, T., Dahlström, P., Henke, N., & Trench, M. (2017). Artificial Intelligence: The Next Digital Frontier? McKinsey Global Institute.

5. Agrawal, A., Gans, J., & Goldfarb, A. (2018). Prediction Machines: The Simple Economics of Artificial Intelligence. Harvard Business Review Press.

6. Tegmark, M. (2017). Life 3.0: Being Human in the Age of Artificial Intelligence. Knopf.

7. Marr, B. (2018). Artificial Intelligence in Practice: How 50 Successful Companies Used AI and Machine Learning to Solve Problems. Wiley.

8. Lee, K. F. (2018). AI Superpowers: China, Silicon Valley, and the New World Order. Houghton Mifflin Harcourt.

9. Brynjolfsson, E., & McAfee, A. (2014). The Second Machine Age: Work, Progress, and Prosperity in a Time of Brilliant Technologies. W. W. Norton & Company.

10. Kaplan, J., & Haenlein, M. (2019). Siri, Siri, in my hand: Who's the fairest in the land? On the interpretations, illustrations, and implications of artificial intelligence. Business Horizons, 62(1), 15-25.

Part 4

1. "Building a StoryBrand: Clarify Your Message So Customers Will Listen" by Donald Miller

2. "The Hero and the Outlaw: Building Extraordinary Brands Through the Power of Archetypes" by Margaret Mark and Carol Pearson

3. "Storynomics: Story-Driven Marketing in the Post-Advertising World" by Robert Mckee and Tom Gerace

4. "Brand Storytelling: Put Customers at the Heart of Your Brand Story" by Miri Rodriguez

5. "Made to Stick: Why Some Ideas Survive and Others Die" by Chip Heath and Dan Heath

6. HBR "Your Strategy Needs a Story" by Martin Reeves, Roland van Straten, Tim Nolan, and Madeleine Michael

Part 5

1. Brown, T. (2009). "Change by Design: How Design Thinking Transforms Organizations and Inspires Innovation." Harper Business.

2. Norman, D. A. (2002). "The Design of Everyday Things." Basic Books.

3. Martin, R. L. (2009). "The Design of Business: Why Design Thinking is the Next Competitive Advantage." Harvard Business Review Press.

4. Kelley, T., & Kelley, D. (2013). "Creative Confidence: Unleashing the Creative Potential Within Us All." Currency.

5. Kolko, J. (2010). "Thoughts on Interaction Design." Elsevier.

6. Brown, T., & Katz, B. (2009). "Change by Design: How Design Thinking Transforms Organizations and Inspires Innovation." Journal of Product Innovation Management, 27(3), 381-383.

7. Norman, D. A. (2004). "Emotional Design: Why We Love (or Hate) Everyday Things." Basic Books.

8. Moggridge, B. (2006). "Designing Interactions." MIT Press.

9. Thaler, R. H., & Sunstein, C. R. (2008). "Nudge: Improving Decisions About Health, Wealth, and Happiness." Yale University Press.

10. Liedtka, J. (2018). "Why Design Thinking Works." Harvard Business Review.

11. McDonough, W., & Braungart, M. (2002). "Cradle to Cradle: Remaking the Way We Make Things." North Point Press.

12. Gaver, W. W. (1991). "Technology affordances." Proceedings of the SIGCHI Conference on Human Factors in Computing Systems, 79-84.

13. Heskett, J. (2002). "Toothpicks and Logos: Design in Everyday Life." Oxford University Press.

14. Kimbell, L. (2011). "Rethinking Design Thinking: Part I." Design and Culture, 3(3), 285-306.

15. Segelström, F., Holmlid, S., & Faste, H. (2009). "Applying User Centered Design to a System Development Project." Designing Inclusive Interactions, 285-294.

16. Cross, N. (2011). "Design Thinking: Understanding How Designers Think and Work." Berg.

17. Kelley, D., & Kelley, T. (2015). "Creative Confidence: Unleashing the Creative Potential Within Us All." Random House.

18. Norman, D. A. (2013). "The Design of Everyday Things: Revised and Expanded Edition." Basic Books.

19. Brown, T. (2008). "Design Thinking." Harvard Business Review, 86(6), 84-92.

20. Hasso Plattner Institute of Design at Stanford University (d.school). (n.d.). "An Introduction to Design Thinking." Retrieved from https://dschool.stanford.edu/

21. Kelley, T., & Kelley, D. (2013). "Creative Confidence: Unleashing the Creative Potential Within Us All." Currency.

22. Thaler, R. H., & Sunstein, C. R. (2008). "Nudge: Improving Decisions About Health, Wealth, and Happiness." Yale University Press.

23. Gaver, W. W. (1991). "Technology affordances." Proceedings of the SIGCHI Conference on Human Factors in Computing Systems, 79-84.

24. Norman, D. A. (2013). "The Design of Everyday Things: Revised and Expanded Edition." Basic Books.

25. Liedtka, J. (2018). "Why Design Thinking Works." Harvard Business Review.

26. Brown, T., & Katz, B. (2009). "Change by Design: How Design Thinking Transforms Organizations and Inspires Innovation." Journal of Product Innovation Management, 27(3), 381-383.

27. Heskett, J. (2002). "Toothpicks and Logos: Design in Everyday Life." Oxford University Press.

28. Kimbell, L. (2011). "Rethinking Design Thinking: Part I." Design and Culture, 3(3), 285-306.

29. Segelström, F., Holmlid, S., & Faste, H. (2009). "Applying User Centered Design to a System Development Project." Designing Inclusive Interactions, 285-294.

30. Cross, N. (2011). "Design Thinking: Understanding How Designers Think and Work." Berg.

31. Brown, T. (2008). "Design Thinking." Harvard Business Review, 86(6), 84-92.

32. Hasso Plattner Institute of Design at Stanford University (d.school). (n.d.).

RANGHAN VENKATRAMAN

What if the well-trodden road of fierce competition doesn't lead to success, but instead molds you into a mere echo of the rivals you strive to surpass? Unveil the paradox of the modern business landscape—a revelation that challenges norms. Enter the realm of B.R.A.N.D., where the key to unlocking future-proof enterprise lies in the uncharted. Are you ready to transcend mediocrity, rewrite the rules, and orchestrate your own symphony of success in the algorithmic age?"